T0274667

"*Parenting with Hope* is the book for parenting teens that we all need! With wisdom and experience, Melissa Kruger offers practical help founded on solid biblical truths. I can see myself revisiting this one again and again!"

—**Hunter Beless**, founder of *Journeywomen*; author of *Read it, See it, Say it, Sing it!* and *Amy Carmichael: The Brown-Eyed Girl Who Learned to Pray*

"Mike and Melissa would be the first to tell you that they are not perfect parents, and that's what makes this book so great. It's about flawed (though very good) parents pointing flawed children to a perfect gospel. Melissa shows you that when you are at the end of your parenting rope, that's when God's promises of grace abound all the more. You, after all, are not writing your kids' story; God is. And that's good news for us all. Having had the chance to pastor two of their kids during their college years, I can commend not only their teaching on parenting, but testify to the fruit. This book is practical and deeply convicting. Our battle against our kids' idols begins in our own hearts! What a gift to the church, and it will be to you also."

—**J.D. Greear**, PhD, pastor, The Summit Church, Raleigh-Durham, NC

"*Parenting with Hope* is a much-needed infusion of gospel-drenched confidence for parents with teenagers."

—**Ruth Chou Simons**, mom to six; *Wall Street Journal* bestselling author, artist, and founder of gracelaced.com

"As a mother on the cusp of raising teens in the coming years, I cherish Melissa's timeless wisdom she generously shares in *Parenting with Hope*. Melissa's words are wrought with deep conviction that God's Word is an unshakable foundation for our lives and our parenting. I'll be returning to this book often for encouragement and practical advice on how to raise my children with my hope fixed on Jesus."

—**Gretchen Sa les**, founder of Well-Watered Women; bestselling author of *The Well-Watered Woman: Rooted in Truth, Growing in Grace, Flourishing in Faith*

parenting
with hope

MELISSA B. KRUGER

HARVEST HOUSE PUBLISHERS
EUGENE, OREGON

Published in association with the literary agency of Wolgemuth & Wilson

Cover design by Faceout Studio, Tim Green

Interior design by Janelle Coury

For bulk, special sales, or ministry purchases, please call 1-800-547-8979.
Email: Customerservice@hhpbooks.com

This logo is a federally registered trademark of the Hawkins Children's LLC. Harvest House Publishers, Inc., is the exclusive licensee of this trademark.

Parenting with Hope

Copyright © 2024 by Melissa B. Kruger
Published by Harvest House Publishers
Eugene, Oregon 97408
www.harvesthousepublishers.com

ISBN 978-0-7369-8626-7 (hardcover)
ISBN 978-0-7369-8627-4 (eBook)

Library of Congress Control Number: 2023938657

Printed in China

23 24 25 26 27 28 29 30 31 32 / RDS / 10 9 8 7 6 5 4 3 2 1

For Mike

*I'm so thankful to be on this
parenting journey with you.
You make home somewhere
I always want to be.*

Contents

Foreword

Emily Jensen and Laura Wifler

If there's one universal feeling in parenting, it's the recurring sense of insecurity as we wonder, *Am I doing this right? Am I teaching my children all that they need to know? Am I using my time with them wisely?* Whether it's the long newborn nights, the active elementary days, or the confusing teen years, parents want to love their children well. But few of us are confident about what that looks like.

As we write this, we stand on the threshold of the teen years. We've passed through the little years, much of the elementary years, and we will soon begin to launch our oldest children into the next stage. As cofounders of Risen Motherhood, a ministry that brings gospel hope to moms, you might think we feel prepared for this. That we have some insider secrets for how to successfully see our children through into adulthood. But that's not the case. If anything, running a ministry has shown us the hardships of parenting, and reinforced our trepidation and apprehension that most parents feel about navigating the teen years.

We're also feeling what everyone told us: Our years in the home with our children are so short. So fun. And so hard. One day, we shared these thoughts with Melissa Kruger, our dear friend and board member for

Risen Motherhood. We were driving in a car, heading to the beach, and asking her for her tips on raising teens. She's a few steps ahead of us in parenting and she had been sharing her wisdom with us. It was in that car that she told us she'd been asked to write a book about parenting teens, but she wasn't sure if she was the right person. We turned to her and simultaneously told her, "You absolutely should. We need that book!"

We're so thankful Melissa not only shared a bit of her wisdom with us that day on the way to the beach, but that she also said yes to sharing her wisdom with you. In these pages, Melissa offers a timeless guide for navigating the labyrinth of the teen years. She's no stranger to the trials and tough questions in this stage of parenting, and her compassionate wisdom and accessible principles fill page after page. But more than helpful principles, Melissa offers us a glorious gift: the gift of knowing and trusting Christ himself. Of staying focused on the grace and help he gives, even in our parenting failures and missteps. If you are like us, you're likely looking ahead to the teen years by looking back at all the ways you didn't do things quite right earlier. But if you are God's, then you are covered by his grace, and you can trust him with both your past and your future. And you can trust him with your teen.

It's because of Jesus we parent with hope.

Emily Jensen and Laura Wifler
Coauthors of *Risen Motherhood* and *Gospel Mom*
Cofounders of Risen Motherhood

Lord, Help Me!

Parenting often feels like a giant roller-coaster ride.

There are slow, uphill, plodding moments. There are fast-paced, downhill, thrilling moments. There are upside-down, I-don't-know-where-I'm-headed moments. Most of all, there are continual twists and turns. Just when you think you know what you're doing and where you're going, the path shifts once again, and you're left breathless with anticipation—as well as trepidation—for what's around the bend.

While parenting in the elementary years, we can easily fall into a settled routine. We gain confidence as healthy patterns emerge, tantrums decrease, sleep schedules normalize, and finally, the children can dress themselves (although, that does not mean socks are matching, or really, anything else, for that matter). It's typically a time of steady and slow plodding while our kids are growing and changing right under our noses. Sometimes, we're so busy getting them to the next sports practice that we don't even really notice how much they're changing.

Suddenly, we find ourselves with preteens, tweens, and teenagers, and it can seem that there are new dangers around every turn. At the same time, we're cresting the peak, with only a few years left of having children in our home. What seemed like a long, steady journey has now sped up precariously and we're feeling as if the ride might be over much too soon.

As we enter the preteen years, we often try to apply all the parenting tools in our toolbox that have worked along the way. However, teens are different than two-year-olds, which means we'll have to find new techniques if we want to create an environment in which they can thrive. As I've made the transition from raising children to tweens, to teens and on to adults, I've had to make shifts to my parenting style. If I were to treat my 22-year-old as though she's 16 and my 16-year-old as though she's 8, I'm going to have problems.

While the need to change course as our children grow older may seem obvious, these parenting transitions snuck up on me along the way, surprising me with unexpected twists and turns. In the early years, I read every book I could find about pregnancy, childbirth, toddlers, and teaching young children to read. However, I didn't find much to help guide me past the early years of mothering. Or maybe I was so busy driving carpool, working, and trying to keep dinner on the table that I started parenting on autopilot. When the family environment started to shift, I hadn't thought through, *What's the best way to navigate this new world of older children? What practices need to change, and what principles stay the same?*

During this season, it's understandable that we may start choosing parenting books that address particular issues we encounter: social media, sex, drugs, rebellion, depression, learning disabilities, discipline, bullying, and teenage stress. And I'm thankful we have specific books on those topics. I've walked the painful journey myself and alongside friends whose teens are struggling through all sorts of teenage issues that have left us on our knees asking God for help. The older the child, the more significant the impact of their decisions (it makes battles about wearing pjs to preschool feel like a fond memory).

If you're entering this stage of parenting, or maybe feeling stuck right in the middle of it, I hope this book will serve as a friendly guide. While I don't have all the answers for every specific situation, I believe there are important and helpful questions for us to consider in this stage of parenting. What are the foundations we need to cling to, and what are the rules we need to relax? How do we discern the difference? How do my own idols—my misplaced desires and affections—impact my parenting? What can we learn from the latest research about teen brain development, and how can that help us understand their behavior? How do we pursue our children relationally? How do we delight in who the Lord is making them to be rather than force them into the mold for what we'd like for them to become? Where can we find help and guidance for the many questions that we have no idea how to answer? How can we support and encourage one another as we parent alongside each other?

As we contemplate these questions, we'll consider principles over prescriptions. This is hard work—it's *heart* work—and we're going to need guidance beyond ourselves. Parenting requires us to rely on God, not simplistic answers. And, this is a continual pursuit, a daily asking for manna in the desert wildernesses of parenting. God is not just at work in your teen's life, he's at work in yours. We need his strength, his guidance, and his grace.

One of the best gifts we can give our children is to root ourselves firmly in Christ, abiding in him for the strength we need.

When it comes to parenting preteens, tweens, and teens, I always think of the first time I learned to drive a stick shift car. My older brother taught me in the parking lot of Morehead Planetarium at UNC-Chapel Hill, and as he did so, I learned what was probably one of the more important lessons I learned in college. In order to make the car go forward, I had to let off the clutch while pressing the gas pedal. If I didn't do these actions simultaneously with just the right timing, the car would stall. If I did them too quickly, the car would lurch forward. I had to get a feel for how much to let my left foot off the clutch while gradually pressing the gas pedal.

As we parent teens, we often want to keep our foot firmly on the brake. However, we have to start giving them gas or they'll never go forward. It's a delicate transition, full of stalls and lurches. Those are to be expected. They are not a sign of your failure as a parent. It's the reality that learning something new takes time.

It's not just our teens who are going through transitions. We're going through them as well. Often, parenting teens brings up our own insecurities, painful memories, and unmet expectations. It's tempting to try to live vicariously through their experiences.

One of the best gifts we can give our children is to root ourselves firmly in Christ, abiding in him for the strength we need. That's why this book is not primarily a how-to guide for parenting teens. It's a book about how to be the parent of a teenager. You're doing this for the first time too. It's okay not to have all the answers and to feel like you don't know what you're doing. We all make mistakes. What we're hoping to do in this book is to consider: *What factors help build a warm and inviting home where faith can flourish?*

As we seek to answer that question, we'll start with the **basics**. The first three chapters will cover foundational principles that are vital for nurturing a home of faith. We'll consider the importance of God's Word, prayer, and the church. You may be tempted to skip these chapters to get to the more "important" questions you're facing, like when to give your teen a phone. Please don't skip these early chapters—they present the essential building blocks for any home of faith.

In the second section we'll consider the **battles** we're facing as parents. And, to be honest, these are probably different than you might assume.

Our greatest battles are not necessarily the cultural wars that surround us, but the idols (anything we trust in more than God) that live in our own hearts. These inward battles may display themselves in different ways in different cultural contexts.

For our context in the West, we'll consider three specific sets of idols: *scholarship and affluence* (idols of power/comfort through achievement), *sports and activities* (idols of approval/power through image) and *social approval and acceptance* (idols of approval/comfort through belonging). Underlying each of these cultural idols are personal source idols (in these chapters, we'll talk more about recognizing them). We'll discuss the need to fight against our own idols in the hopes of creating a home where teens can thrive. Too often, we mistakenly believe we have the power to determine our children's future and the wisdom to know what is best for them.

In the final section of the book, we'll consider the **blessings** we can offer to our children. We'll consider three *A*'s: *acceptance* (a home of grace), *availability* (a home of welcome), and *affection* (a home of warmth). By building on the basics and battling against our idols, we can richly bless our children.

I want to encourage you: While the teen years can be difficult, they can also be so much fun. I've always enjoyed teenagers. I majored in secondary math education and taught at a large public high school. Each year I encountered 150 different students. They had a variety of backgrounds, personalities, and personal struggles. While they were all different, they all needed to know that I cared about them as individuals, not just that I wanted to teach them about math. I found I had to win them relationally before I could engage them intellectually. This didn't mean that I tried to be their friend or never gave them homework. They needed boundaries and discipline, but most importantly, they needed love.

Many of the principles I learned while teaching high schoolers apply to parenting. Every child is different, but certain styles of teaching and parenting have better outcomes. We can learn from the research and wisdom of those who have studied these concepts. We want to begin in God's

Word and consider how its principles apply to our children. We can also learn from the insights and research of those who have studied teen development. For that reason, each chapter of this book is broken into three sections:

- Principles for Parents: Thinking Biblically
- Purposeful Parenting: Engaging Gracefully
- Practical Advice: Living Wisely

In the first section, we'll consider what we need to understand about each topic from a biblical perspective. Then we'll think through how to apply those principles into purposeful parenting. In the last section, I'll share practical advice from a variety of sources—including wisdom from Christians as well as helpful research from teen brain experts, modern psychologists, and social scientists.

There's also a study guide available for this book. I highly recommend using it as you read this book—it will give you the opportunity to pause and reflect upon biblical passages as you consider how to apply these principles in your home. In the study guide, you'll also find questions that are great for group discussions. I encourage you to read this book in community. Grab some friends and talk about these concepts together. It can be more difficult to do this while parenting older children. While every mom or dad of a two-year-old knows the feeling of dealing with tantrums, you may feel isolated because of what you're facing with your teen. You may feel more alone and unsure of your parenting than you ever did during the younger years. You most likely will have to limit what you share to protect your teen.

However, you may be surprised to find that other parents are struggling just like you. The issues they face in their home might be different, but they are searching for wisdom and struggling with insecurity as well. I've talked to so many parents of teens who feel alone in this journey. Take the time to dig into the basics, pray for one another in your battles, and work together to find creative ways to build a home of blessing for your teens.

A few weeks ago, I was talking to a friend about this book, telling her I didn't know how to begin. She has adult children who have children of their own. She looked at me with the wisdom of a sage and didn't miss a beat:

"'Lord, help me!' That is how you should begin."

I think she's right.

Lord, help me. Lord, help us. Let's begin.

—Melissa Kruger

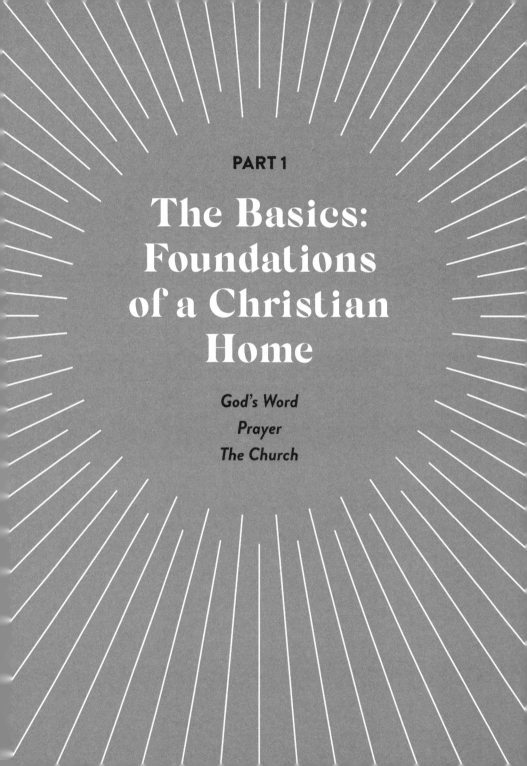

PART 1

The Basics:
Foundations
of a Christian
Home

God's Word
Prayer
The Church

CHAPTER 1

An Instruction Manual for Life: God's Word

I'll never forget the first time I put my daughter Emma in her car seat. My husband and I were living in Edinburgh, Scotland, and Emma was born a week early. As we prepared to leave the hospital, we bundled her up and strapped her in the seat to the best of our abilities. She looked so incredibly tiny in her big baby carrier.

We then called for a taxi. Living overseas on a student budget meant that we didn't have a car, so I'd never had an opportunity to practice adjusting a car seat. As we carried all our things to the waiting driver, we did our best to safely secure her, feeling completely unprepared and unqualified for the task before us.

Buckling her in was just the beginning of my feelings of inadequacy. I didn't know how to bathe her, feed her, care for her, or parent her. I'd been handed this amazing gift and I found myself wondering, *Don't they come with instruction manuals or something?*

I'd read the books; I'd tried to prepare. But head knowledge can take you only so far. There are some parts of parenting that are learned only as you put theory into practice.

I felt inadequate on my first day of parenting. I continue to feel that way 23 years later. While I've now been a mother for many years, I'm still the first-time mother of an adult daughter. I'm still learning. I'm still growing. I'm still making mistakes. I'm still finding my way.

While I haven't found that longed-for parenting manual that gives me explicit instructions for each season of parenting, I can tell you, without a doubt, that I've found something even better. God's Word has been my firm anchor, my shining light, my faithful guide, my trusted resource, and my sure hope in every season of parenting.

It hasn't told me the particulars of how to get my child to sleep through the night or eat her vegetables. However, it has imbued me with patience and kindness while enduring another sleepless night or finding a veggie mysteriously hidden under a napkin (again). God's Word hasn't kept me (or my children) from the realities of suffering, but it has been a comfort while walking through painful losses and unmet expectations. God's Word doesn't promise me that my children will live long lives, get married, have grandchildren, or become Christians, but it does promise me that God will be with me always, never leaving nor forsaking me.

 **What we believe and how we live matters greatly for whether our children know, love, and obey God's Word.**

As we enter the preteen and teenage years with our children, we know God's Word is important. We want them to read it. We encourage them to study it. We hope that they'll love it. And we pray with all sorts of fervor that they'll obey it.

But before we get to our children's relationship with God's Word, I want us to think as parents about *our* relationship with God and his Word. What we believe and how we live matters greatly for whether our children know, love, and obey God's Word. We can't make our children believe in Jesus (see Ephesians 2:8-10), but we can put them in an environment that allows them to witness the fruit of God's work in our lives. We can hope they hear God's Word in our home and see its effects on our lives.

You may be tempted to skip over these first chapters, wanting to move on to the "important" stuff—like telling you whether or not it's okay for your teens to watch certain YouTube videos or wear certain kinds of clothing.

There's a reason we're starting here. Parenting isn't just about figuring out how to manage your teen. In every season of parenting, God is teaching us about himself. He's parenting us as we parent our children. He's teaching us as we teach them. He walks with us and wants us to rely on him for the wisdom we so desperately long for as parents.

I can't promise you a ready resource guide to all of life's answers for parenting teens. But I can lead you to the One who has the answers, the wisdom, and the guidance you need for your particular child. Thankfully, he promises to be with you and guide you. And, we find him in his Word.

Principles for Parents: Thinking Biblically

Moses, the servant of God, led the Israelites out of slavery in Egypt on their way to the Promised Land. While wandering in the wilderness, he taught the Israelites the importance of following God and teaching their children to do the same. He instructed them generationally:

> Now this is the commandment—the statutes and the rules— that the LORD your God commanded me to teach you, that you may do them in the land to which you are going over, to possess it, that you may fear the LORD your God, you and your son and your son's son, by keeping all his statutes and his commandments, which I command you, all the days of your life...
>
> Hear, O Israel: The LORD our God, the LORD is one. You

shall love the Lord your God with all your heart and with all your soul and with all your might. And these words that I command you today shall be on your heart. You shall teach them diligently to your children, and shall talk of them when you sit in your house, and when you walk by the way, and when you lie down, and when you rise. You shall bind them as a sign on your hand, and they shall be as frontlets between your eyes. You shall write them on the doorposts of your house and on your gates (Deuteronomy 6:1-9).

This passage encourages us as parents to teach our children diligently—as we sit and rise and go along the way. However, it doesn't *start* with us teaching them.

It starts with us learning about God ourselves.

We are to love the Lord with all our might. We're to have his commands on our heart. We're to obey his Word and fear him. If we don't have this foundation, we'll never be able to teach our children.

All relationships take time to build. Friends plan times to get together and catch up. Spouses reconnect on date nights. Church members chat over potluck dinners. Building fellowship with others takes time. If we want to grow a friendship with God, we need time in his presence for that relationship to flourish. Reading the Bible on a daily basis allows us the opportunity to get to know God: What does he care about? How does he respond? Who does he love?

And, the more we know God, the more we will love God.

Have you ever had the experience of meeting someone, really enjoying them, but after a few weeks, the shine starts to wear off in the relationship? The deeper you get to know most people, the more you might be disinclined to like them. We've all got issues and problems and annoying habits. At times, this can make us fearful of letting anyone really know us or getting to know others.

However, it's the complete opposite with God. The more we know him—truly know him—the more wonderful he is. He's the creator of all that's good. Everything that you think is wonderful, beautiful, magnificent, amazing…God is the author. All that is good in this world reflects his goodness.

Psalm 19:1-2 tells us, "The heavens declare the glory of God, and the sky above proclaims his handiwork. Day to day pours out speech, and night to night reveals knowledge." All of creation showcases his glory.

Yet, there's something even better than natural revelation to teach us about God—his Word. Psalm 19 continues, "The law of the LORD is perfect, reviving the soul; the testimony of the LORD is sure, making wise the simple; the precepts of the LORD are right, rejoicing the heart; the commandment of the LORD is pure, enlightening the eyes" (Psalm 19:7-8).

Go back and read those verses again. What parent doesn't want revival and refreshment? Or wisdom? Or joy? Or enlightenment? What we most desperately want as parents isn't found in a spa vacation or the newest self-help book or even the bestselling Christian author's next amazing book. It's found in God's Word.

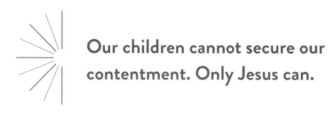

Our children cannot secure our contentment. Only Jesus can.

Here's the reality—if we're going to walk through the teenage years with love, joy, peace, patience, kindness, goodness, faithfulness, gentleness, and self-control, it's found in only one place. We have to abide in Jesus. And have his words abide in us. There's no other way. Let me repeat that statement: *There's no other way to bear fruit except abiding in Jesus.* Even if your teen breezed through these years with straight *A*'s, was captain of the football team, and voted prom king, you wouldn't have peace or joy without Jesus. Our children cannot secure our contentment. Only Jesus can.

I love to garden. I'm always amazed as I watch the tomatoes slowly grow on the vine. I spend the summer enjoying the produce. By the end of fall, the first freeze comes, and it's time to clear out the old vines.

It's easy work because once vines are dead, they lose all their strength and break apart with little effort. A detached vine crumbles to dust with the slightest touch. Perhaps that's why Jesus chose to use the image of a vine when he commanded us to abide in him, warning that apart from him, we can do nothing (John 15:1-6). Our best parenting efforts will crumble to dust without the soul-strengthening power of time spent abiding in the Word and prayer.

Parenting tweens and teens is difficult. They are dealing with changes to their bodies, swirling emotions, and fluctuating hormones. They can be awkward or angry; shy or stubborn; tearful or theatrical—and that's all in one day.

You'll be tempted to look for your joy in your children's happiness. To find your peace in their success. To be kind when they obey. To be gentle when they are loving. To love when they make you proud. To desperately just want for them to be okay. And, of course you want good things for your children and rightly rejoice in their happiness.

However, our children cannot be the source of our contentment. It's an unfair and impossible burden to place on them. Consider the pressure it puts on a child if they think they are responsible for your happiness. We're tempted to put the same pressure on our spouses. Asking anyone else to secure our happiness always leaves us unfulfilled and those we love overburdened.

Only the fruit of the Spirit at work in our heart can produce the fruit of true joy and peace and love. Yes, we can delight in our children and rejoice in good circumstances with them, but they need us to find our strength and security from a different source. We love our children freely when we're firmly rooted in Jesus.

Psalm 1 tells us that the person who delights in the law of the Lord is like a "a tree planted by streams of water that yields its fruit in its season, and its leaf does not wither. *In all that he does, he prospers*" (verse 3, emphasis added).

Jeremiah uses this same imagery and declares, "Blessed is the man who trusts in the Lord, whose trust is the Lord. He is like a tree planted by water, that sends out its roots by the stream, and does not fear when heat comes, for its leaves remain green, and is not anxious in the year of drought, *for it does not cease to bear fruit*" (Jeremiah 17:7-8, emphasis added).

If we want to be parents who prosper in every season, we need to root ourselves in God's Word—trusting in it, delighting in it, meditating upon it. Think of that tree planted by a stream. It's independent of nature's droughts and the sun's heat. It bears fruit regardless of circumstances because it has an unending source from which to drink. We want to be like that tree.

Every parent has a unique set of circumstances as they parent. You may be concerned about the influences of culture on your child. Your child may be addicted to alcohol, drugs, video games, social media, or pornography. Your child might be battling anxiety or depression or suicidal thoughts. Your child might be engaged in sexual sin or lying or stealing or bullying. Your child might be making straight *A*'s and doing everything right, but pridefully independent of any need for God. Your child may not want to go to church or have spiritual conversations. Your child may be lonely or socially awkward, vulnerable to the harmful words of others. Your child may be starving herself in a quest to be beautiful (as the world defines it) and belong. Your child may be struggling in school or be cut from her favorite sports team.

I know wonderful Christian parents who have dealt with every one of these situations. We don't get to control the hardships our children suffer. We don't get to choose the mistakes they make. We don't get to pick the battles they will fight.

However, we can choose to be parents who find our strength in the Lord, not our children's successes or well-being. This is a gift to our teens and releases them of a huge burden. We can seek God for wisdom when we have no idea what to do in the circumstances we are given rather than attempting to control circumstances ourselves. We can ask him for strength when we face the unthinkable or endure the unimaginable. In the midst of suffering, we can look to his Word for joy and comfort and peace. Our parenting prospers not because of our perfection (or our children's), but because of God's power. It's his grace and nothing else.

Purposeful Parenting: Engaging Gracefully

We begin building our homes on God's Word by abiding in it ourselves on a daily basis. Then we're ready to teach it to our children, engaging them with the truths we are learning for ourselves. We can do this through our example, our habits, and our daily conversations.

Our Example

Here's the good news/bad news as we share our faith with our children. According to a national sociological study of American religious parents (not just Christian parents):

> Parental consistency in word and deed, rules, and meaningful intentions affects the success of religious transmission to children. Perception of hypocrisy when parents do not act in congruence with their religious teachings, or when parents follow the letter but not the meaning of the law…reduce children's interests in carrying forward the religious faith and practices of their parents.[1]

How we live affects what our children believe about God. Take a moment to pause and consider the weightiness of that truth (yes, it's somewhat overwhelming to consider).

At the same time, let me clarify: *Your actions are unable to save your child.* Salvation is a free gift of God's grace, not the result of parental perfection. However, God uses providential means to save people. It is a blessing for children to grow up in a home where the fruit of faith is readily apparent. Religious training through families is often the agent of grace by which our children come to faith. God is the one saving, but our homes are opportunities to create a healthy environment for spiritual truths to flourish.

Our homes can also create a negative environment. If our actions don't match our words, our hypocrisy will adversely affect our children. Teens can spot a fake. If we claim to love God but are filled with anger, discontentment, lying, and impatience, our children will notice. If we bow down to the idols of money, success, power, approval, comfort, or control, our children will observe the truth of what we love. And, most likely they will love and serve the same idols we do.

Let me also clarify: This doesn't mean that prodigal children are the result of a lack of parental integrity. I know many wonderful Christ-honoring parents whose children are not walking with the Lord. We have to hold the uncomfortable tension of two parallel truths: Our personal integrity as we walk with Jesus matters for our children, but is unable to save them. Our hypocrisy and idolatry will have a negative impact on our children, but ultimately, a lack of parental integrity is not the cause of prodigal children.

Where does this leave us? The first thing that comes to my mind is the old hymn "Trust and Obey." We entrust our children to the Lord for salvation and we obey the Lord, hoping that our faithful example will leave an indelible impact on our children. We also do everything we can to creatively engage our children with God's Word, because it has the power to do what we cannot: transform our children's minds and make them wise for salvation (Romans 12:2; 2 Timothy 3:15).

Our Habits

Every home has daily habits. You've formed them, and you probably don't even think about them very much at this point. Hopefully by the teenage years (with the exception of children with special needs), your children brush their teeth twice a day, dress themselves, comb their hair, and take showers on a regular basis (although some teenage boys might struggle with these last two). Your home has given them daily rhythms.

One of the habits that we tried to instill early in our home was daily Bible reading. When our children were young, we read a Bible story with them every night before bedtime. Once they entered the elementary years, we began having a devotional time every morning before they went to school. This habit has continued into the teen years. Surprisingly, my kids have never complained about this time together as a family, which has taught me a lot. Here are some of the lessons I've learned.

Begin Early

The earlier you begin habits, the better for your children. Just think how problematic it would be if you forgot to teach your children to brush their teeth until they were age five. They'd probably already have a few cavities, and they wouldn't have this habit fixed in their daily routine. (And, just as a side note, I did forget to teach my youngest daughter to brush her teeth in the morning. She came home from school one day and said, "Mom, I didn't know people brushed their teeth in the morning too!" This is what can happen to the last child.)

The earlier you can begin a daily habit of reading the Bible with your children, the better. Here's the secret I tell myself on a regular basis: *Kids only know the family life you make normal for them.* Most likely, my kids have never really wondered if other families spend five to ten minutes each morning for a devotional. They may be surprised at how few of their friends read the Bible regularly with their parents. That's okay. You get to create the habits in your home.

If you feel like you've waited too long and now your children are too old to begin, I encourage you to start with a conversation. I've found that if you begin from a place of invitation rather than compulsion, the conversation usually goes better. Something like: "I want to ask you all to try something with me for a few weeks. Could we commit together as a family to be at the breakfast table ten minutes before you leave for school so that we can read the Bible and pray for one another? I know you may not want to do this, or it may feel strange as we begin, but I believe it would be a blessing for our family to have this time together. I love you all, and I've been learning how important God's Word is, and I want us to learn from it together. If mornings are too difficult, can you help me to think of a good time that we could do this as a family?"

As your children become teens, it's helpful to allow them to become stakeholders in the family habits. Invite them into the discussion. Ask for their input. Engage them graciously. During these years, it's vital to involve them and listen to their perspective.

Kids only know the family life you make normal for them.

Also, prepare for the discussion to go differently than you may want it to. Recently, I asked my teens if we could do a family Bible study together once a week. They looked at me with eyebrows raised and asked, "Why would we do that?" I told them some of my reasons, and they responded, "We don't want to do that; we already know how to study the Bible." After some further back-and-forth discussions, I jokingly called them all pagans for not wanting to study with me, and we left it at that. Bible reading is serious business, but you don't have to take yourself too seriously. If at first you don't succeed, keep trying with new ideas. Pray for wisdom and insight as you continually invite your children to the goodness of God's Word.

Engage Warmly

Centuries ago, Puritan pastor John James encouraged, "Let your warmest affection, your greatest cheerfulness, your most engaging smiles, be put on when you teach Scriptural truths to your children."[2] He understood that *how* we teach our children matters in their receptivity toward *what* we are teaching them. Modern research agrees. According to a recent study, parents with warm and nurturing relationships were more likely to pass on their faith and religious practices to their children.[3]

Basically, don't make reading the Bible a miserable experience for your kids. It just doesn't go well if you're frustrated and yelling at everyone to "COME AND READ THE BIBLE!" Create healthy patterns, but don't get stuck on some sort of idyllic image of perfection. Every family is different. You may decide to read the Bible together once a week on Sundays. That's great. It's better to create a warm and inviting environment of engagement once a week than to have everyone sitting at the table every morning learning nothing because they all feel scolded and miserable. The goal is to create habits that allow your kids to learn God's Word. Focus on what works well for your family and how they learn best, not the particular method or timing if they're reluctant. Be creative for your family (you don't have to do what other people are doing) and ask God for wisdom.

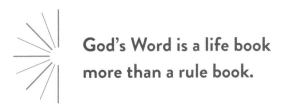

God's Word is a life book
more than a rule book.

While there will always be a recalcitrant teenager who doesn't want to talk about spiritual matters, during my years of teaching I found that most teenagers are longing for adult attention and conversation. They may act like they don't want it, but I've found our availability as adults deeply matters to teens. Ask questions more than you supply easy answers. Be interested in their thoughts and show respect for their ideas. These kinds of regular interactions open the door for further conversations at other times of the day. You may be surprised to find that your teens enjoy these times together, however reluctant they may be in the beginning.

I've also found that how we think about the Bible affects how we communicate it to our children. Some people think of the Bible simply as a rule book—a burden that shows them all the ways they've failed. However, God's Word is a life book more than a rule book. It's a grace to us, a demonstration of God's kindness and pursuit of his people. Scripture is a tutor, showing us our inability to fulfill the law perfectly as a means of leading us to Christ. Yes, the Bible teaches us what not to do. But more importantly, it teaches us what *to do* in order to have abundant life.

If you share God's Word more often with your children in corrective ways ("Don't do this!") than in comforting ways ("God is your refuge and help!"), they may be less inclined to want to read it. Allow your teaching of God's Word to be full of the good news: "Yes, you need a Savior. Let me tell you about how amazing Jesus is and how much he loves you."

Personal Habits

We all want opportunities to talk with our teens about the Bible. However, we also want them to be reading it for themselves. One of the best ways to normalize daily Bible reading for our children is for them to see us reading our Bibles regularly. Our personal habits leave such a deep impression on them.

I've never told my children explicitly, "You need to read your Bible on your own every day." But I've watched as they've slowly implemented these habits into their lives. In the teen years, it's important that your kids start developing their own time in the Bible at their own pace. We want them to develop a relationship with God, not guilt them or nag them into reading their Bibles. I encourage you to give each of your tweens or teens their own Bible, provide helpful Bible study resources and devotionals, and then pray that your children will open their Bibles and start reading on their own.

Our Conversations

Moses instructed the Israelites, "You shall teach them diligently to your children, and shall talk of them when you sit in your house, and when you walk by the way, and when you lie down, and when you rise" (Deuteronomy 6:7). When we read God's Word regularly, it naturally overflows into our conversations with our children. Let me encourage you: Look for opportunities to talk about God as you go throughout your day with your children. Learning about God isn't something that happens only during family devotions or private Bible reading. Learning about God is done in community, as we are living our lives.

Listen to your teens as they discuss the circumstances of their day. Avoid jumping in and offering quick solutions or simplistic answers. Don't minimize what might be a discouraging or difficult situation for them. Ask good questions, engage them in conversation, and help them learn how to process their circumstances through a biblical lens. You want to help them develop discernment for themselves, not just thoughtlessly follow rules. In the teen years, it's important (and sometimes difficult!) for parents to be quick to listen, slow to speak (James 1:19).

The survey findings from *Handing Down the Faith* explain:

> The most effective parent conversations about religion with children are children-centered rather than parent-centered. In them, children ask questions and talk more while parents mostly listen; the questions about religion are clearly related to the children's lives; parents try to help children understand their religious faith and practices; the conversations are open, not rigid or highly controlled; and the larger relationship between parents and children is thereby nurtured. When parents, by contrast, talk too much, make demands without explanations, force unwanted conversations, and restrict discussions to topics that they control, faith transmission to children is likely to be ineffective or counterproductive.[4]

The tween and teen years are a wonderful opportunity to understand the spiritual development of our children. While you may think that these are the last few years of opportunity for you to teach them all your hard-earned wisdom, they actually learn better as they talk *with* you rather than hear lectures from you. Diligence in our conversations with them doesn't mean we are the ones doing all the talking. It means that we are always thinking about ways to allow the Word to saturate our conversations and the advice we offer.

When my children were young, there were multiple cookbooks that taught various ways to sneak extra vegetables into foods like lasagnas, soups, and brownies without children knowing. The concept was to smuggle healthy foods into the foods the kids already loved so that they would get the veggies they needed.

This is a helpful way to think about working God's Word into our daily conversations with our children. You may not always be able to quote the exact verse, but as you have God's Word hidden in your own heart, you'll be able to offer his wisdom in the midst of driving your teen to soccer practice, waiting in the doctor's office, or having a late-night conversation.

Practical Advice: Living Wisely

My college education courses introduced me to the concept of different parenting styles (which were applicable to teaching styles as well), and we'll continue to refer to these throughout the book. While modern psychology is limited in its ability to give us ultimate wisdom, we can glean common-grace insights from its research. Understanding these different parenting styles has been helpful to me as I've sought to teach my children to love and obey God's Word.

Essentially, there are four different types of parenting: authoritarian, authoritative, permissive, and uninvolved/negligent.[5] Here's a helpful way to categorize these styles:

Authoritarian parents tend to have high expectations and demands, with low levels of warmth, responsiveness, and acceptance. They could also be called *domineering parents*, who lead by intimidation and fear.

Authoritative parents tend to have high expectations and demands, with high levels of warmth, responsiveness, and acceptance. They could also be called *shepherding parents*, who lead wisely with patience and gentleness.

Permissive parents tend to have low expectations and demands, with high levels of warmth, responsiveness, and acceptance. They could also be called *indulgent parents*, who follow their children's lead and desires.

Uninvolved or negligent parents tend to have low expectations and demands, with low levels of warmth, responsiveness, and acceptance. They could also be called *absentee parents*, whose impact is felt by their absence more than their presence.

When it comes to understanding the distinctions between these different parenting styles, I find it helpful to imagine a backyard play area.

An authoritarian/domineering parent sets up a pack 'n play in the midst of a big yard and restricts the child to playing in that small and confined area. That setup may work when the child is young, but eventually the child will outgrow the pack 'n play and become increasingly frustrated by its constraints and limitations.

The authoritative/shepherd parent builds a fence that encloses the yard and allows the child a wide area to play and run that is age appropriate.

The permissive/indulgent parent opens the door to the unfenced backyard and says, "Have fun playing outside!"

The uninvolved/absentee parent has no idea what the child is doing or where the child is.

While these images present a somewhat simplistic understanding of these parenting styles, they provide insight into our homes. It's helpful to consider the type of home you grew up in, as well as your tendencies as a

Permissive
Indulgent Parent

"You're in charge"

Low expectations, high warmth,
little oversight, lenient

Lets the child lead

Typical source idols:
comfort and approval

Asks: What does my child want?

Authoritative
Shepherd Parent

"Let's have a conversation"

Warmth, affection, high
expectations, consequences, clear
standards, responsive, attentive

Prioritizes child's needs and abilities

Leads with patience,
gentleness, curiosity

Fights source idols and seeks
to honor God in parenting

Asks: What does God
want for my child?

HIGH

WARMTH

EXPECTATIONS

LOW   HIGH

Negligent
Absentee Parent

"I'm not getting involved"

Low expectations, low warmth,
absent, neglectful, passive,
uninterested, uninvolved

Doesn't lead

Any of the four source idols could
lead to negligent parenting

Doesn't ask

Authoritarian
Domineering Parent

"I'm in charge"

High expectations and
demands, controlling

Directive more than relational

Low warmth, responsiveness,
and affection

Leads by intimidation and fear

Typical source idols:
control and success

Asks: What do I want
from/for my child?

LOW

parent. When it comes to raising our children to love and obey God, we want to have rules and boundaries for them that reflect those found in God's Word (that's the fence we put up). It's loving and kind for us to give them wise boundaries.

However, we have to be careful that we don't keep our tweens and teens in boundaries that are too restrictive (like the pack 'n play) and are more about our fears rather than God's Word. We also have to guard against having no boundaries at all because we fear that may cause our children to not like us. And, as for the uninvolved/absentee category, I'm thinking that if you are reading this book, you probably aren't a negligent parent. So, for most of our discussions, I'll focus on the authoritarian, authoritative, and permissive parenting styles.

Both authoritarian/domineering and permissive/indulgent parenting are associated with negative outcomes for children. Children from authoritarian homes have lower academic performance, poorer social skills, and higher rates of mental illness, drug abuse, and delinquency. Children from permissive homes have higher rates of impulsive and egocentric behavior, poorer social skills, and problematic relationships. In contrast, children from authoritative/shepherding homes have higher academic performance, better social skills, less mental illness, and lower rates of delinquency.[6] In addition, children who grow up in an authoritative/shepherding environment are more likely to consider the faith of their parents an important part of their own life.[7] While parenting styles are not ultimately determinative for outcomes, they are a helpful tool for evaluating best practices as parents.

We want to teach God's Word to our children as the absolute authority in their lives. It's the firm fence for which we can always plead with our children, "Stay in this boundary for your good!" However, every family will have additional rules within their home. It takes a combination of wisdom and prayer to know how to formulate our home rules, as well as enforce them. In our next chapter, which is about prayer, we'll discuss this concept more as we seek God's wisdom in the ways we discuss and determine helpful boundaries for our teens.

A Note of Gospel Hope

Sometimes, it's intimidating to teach God's Word to our teens. Perhaps you feel as though you don't know it very well. Maybe you feel guilty for the ways you didn't obey your parents or God as a teenager and you feel like you can't expect your children to do what you didn't do. Perhaps you fear that you'll talk about the Bible too much and they'll become disinterested. Or, maybe you have many doubts yourself and are concerned your teens will ask questions you can't answer.

Let me encourage you today—it's okay to have questions. It's okay to still be learning. It's okay to be unsure of yourself. None of us feels up to the task! Thankfully we're not alone. The Spirit guides us in all truth, and God brings other Christians into our lives who can offer additional wisdom and insight for our questions. Teach the biblical truth you know, read the Bible yourself, talk with your children about the questions you have, ask a pastor or teacher for help finding answers, entrust your fears to God, and teach your children that God's grace is big enough for all their failings (and yours too!). Small steps of faithfulness can lead to big changes in our homes. Keep depending on God's Word and his wisdom in your own life, and that will impact your children.

God loves you. He loves your teen. Today is a new opportunity to know Jesus better. May his grace guide you, protect you, and help you!

MK

Parenting Principles to Ponder

- Spending time in God's Word matters. It nourishes our souls as parents and prepares us to share with our teens.

- Teens learn about godly practices by our example and our conversations with them.

- Parents who provide authoritative/shepherding homes have high expectations, alongside high levels of warmth and responsiveness. These homes typically have the best outcomes for teens.

CHAPTER 2

The Power of His Presence: Prayer

After getting Emma buckled into the Edinburgh taxi (whew!), we arrived back at our small one-bedroom flat. I looked around our space with new eyes. We had left a few days before as a couple. Now, we returned as parents. All the months and weeks of preparation didn't seem like enough. I had no idea what to do with this baby. So, I started by pulling out her changing mat. That seemed like an important (and needed) first step.

About an hour after we got home, another taxi pulled up to our flat. It was my mom. I don't think I've ever been so happy to see someone in my life! Originally, she planned to arrive before Emma's birth. However, with Emma coming a week early, she providentially arrived at the exact moment I needed her most. It was like Mary Poppins had walked in the door, adept and able to help me with everything I had no idea how to do.

It's one thing to have books to tell us what to do. It's another thing to have someone present to help us. I asked my mom so many questions I'd never thought to ask her before. *How do I bathe her? Why is she so fussy? Do you think that's a tired cry or a wet cry or a hungry cry? What can I do to help her sleep better?*

As our children enter the teen years, I think we all wish we had someone right there beside us, telling us: "Don't say anything about that mismatched outfit today." "It's okay that he didn't make that sports team—he may be disappointed today, but it's going to work out." "She's not really angry at you; she just had a bad day." "I know he didn't want to talk about it; that's normal. Sometimes teenage boys don't know how to communicate their feelings."

Wouldn't it be nice if we had some sort of Alexa device, ready and waiting to answer all our questions about what to do with our teenagers? Or maybe a live-in advisor to help guide us and keep us from making mistakes and saying all the wrong things?

Like nothing else in my life, motherhood has helped me to realize my limitations. I couldn't make my baby nurse. I couldn't stop her from crying. I couldn't get her to fall asleep. I often had no idea what to do.

During the teen years, we're all facing issues that seem much bigger than figuring out how to nurse or finding ways to help our baby fall asleep (although a desperate and sleep-deprived new mom may feel differently). We recognize our lack of wisdom and know we need help, but sometimes we don't know where to turn.

While we don't have someone physically beside us telling us everything we may want to know, we do have help. We can cry out to God, asking him to do what we are powerless to do. We have the Spirit within us, who promises to guide us and lead us. We can pray with the psalmist, "Teach me to do your will, for you are my God! Let your good Spirit lead me on level ground!" (Psalm 143:10).

In my own life, when problems arise with my children, usually I talk first to my husband, asking what he thinks. Then I turn to trusted friends, seeking their thoughts on the matter. I may do some internet research, trying to figure out what is normal or age appropriate. I'll talk to an older mom and ask her advice. I may read a book on the topic.

When I've extinguished all my options and find myself at a loss for what to do, it will finally occur to me: *Have I even prayed about this? Have I asked God to show me what is best?* Too often, I'm quick to look for answers on my own, without ever asking God to help me find them. While I don't believe the maxim "God helps those who helps themselves," I often live as though I do.

Thankfully, God is patient with my slowness to learn. I can't tell you the number of times (after I finally got on my knees and prayed about the situation) he has worked in amazing ways. It might not have been that my situation changed, but perhaps I felt more at peace. Or perhaps the sermon that week happened to speak to my heart in just the way I needed to hear. Or maybe I ran into a friend and we discovered we were both struggling with the same issue, and she offered excellent advice.

When we pray, we'll find a double blessing—because prayer is about more than getting answers. It's about entering into joy.

God is there for us. He is ready to give us wisdom. James promises, "If any of you lacks wisdom, let him ask God, who gives generously to all without reproach, and it will be given him" (James 1:5). Did you read that good news? We can ask God. It doesn't bother him if we pray and ask him for wisdom at 8:00 a.m. and then again at 8:05 a.m. And then again at 9:00 a.m. He's got all the wisdom of the universe, and he's ready to give generously. All we have to do is ask.

Prayer is a gift we often neglect. As Tim Keller writes, "A triune God would call us to converse with him…because he wants to share the joy he has. Prayer is our way of entering into the happiness of God himself."[1] And when we pray, we'll find a double blessing—because prayer is about more than getting answers. It's about entering into joy.

Principles for Parents: Thinking Biblically

All throughout the Bible, God's people pray. Isaac prayed for Rebekah to conceive (Genesis 25:21). Moses prayed for deliverance for the Israelites (Numbers 21:7). Hannah prayed and wept, asking for a child (1 Samuel 1:10). Samuel prayed for the people of God, while teaching them what was good and right (1 Samuel 12:23). Hezekiah prayed for healing (2 Kings 20:5). Solomon prayed for wisdom (1 Kings 3:9). Daniel prayed three times a day to God despite a king's edict against doing so (Daniel 6:10). The Psalms are essentially a book of prayers, teaching us how to pour our hearts out to God in both our sorrows and our joys.

Paul prayed for the churches—for their love of God to abound (Philippians 1:9), for spiritual wisdom and understanding (Colossians 1:9), for opportunities to witness (Colossians 4:3), for their walk to be worthy of the gospel (2 Thessalonians 1:11), and in hopes that he might see them face to face (1 Thessalonians 3:10).

God's people are praying people. We understand we need God's help. As parents, we have the high calling to pray for our children.

Jesus: Our Example to Follow

Most importantly, Jesus prayed. And he taught us to pray. As we think about our need to pray as parents of teens, the Lord's prayer can instruct us and guide us.

In the book of Matthew, Jesus taught his disciples:

> When you pray, do not heap up empty phrases as the Gentiles do, for they think that they will be heard for their many words. Do not be like them, for your Father knows what you need before you ask him. Pray then like this:
>
> > "Our Father in heaven,
> > hallowed be your name.
> > Your kingdom come,

your will be done,
   on earth as it is in heaven.
Give us this day our daily bread,
and forgive us our debts,
   as we also have forgiven our debtors.
And lead us not into temptation,
   but deliver us from evil" (Matthew 6:7-13).

This model prayer offers so many lessons we can learn as parents. Let's consider a few.

Who do we pray to?

We begin by praying to "Our Father." God understands parental love. We get to enter his presence as a beloved child, welcomed and accepted. We also belong to a family, the church (notice the collective "our" Father). This passage reminds us it's not necessary to say long, eloquent, or impressive prayers, for God already knows what we need. But he still wants us to come and talk to him. Our prayers matter. God reigns from heaven; he's ruling and able to help. While you may feel like all the burdens and responsibilities of your family rest on you as the parent, it's God who is the ultimate parent. He cares when we cry out to him.

While you may feel like all the burdens and responsibilities of your family rest on you as the parent, it's God who is the ultimate parent. He cares when we cry out to him.

What do we pray about?

Jesus began his prayer by reminding us of our priorities and reorienting our desires. Most of us jump right to the circumstantial need of the moment (and God cares about those as well). However, Jesus started by teaching us to pray for something more glorious: "Hallowed be your name." He reminds us to pray what is most important, what is most needed: May God's name be declared holy throughout the earth. God's glory is always to be at the top of our prayer list.

Jesus then taught us to pray for God's kingdom to come and his will to be done. Take a moment to think about what it means to pray, "Your will be done." We're not in the driver's seat when it comes to knowing what's best for our children. Our prayers that they get asked to the prom or make the soccer team or get into the college of their choice or find a group of Christian friends (all good things) might not be God's plan for our children. As we pray, "Your will be done," we are relinquishing our desires (and acknowledging the limitations of our understanding) and asking that God would do what is best. We entrust our longings to him, knowing this: "If the good thing we desire is good for us, we shall have it. If it is not good, then the not having is good for us."[2]

At the same time, Jesus taught us to pray for our daily bread. We can ask him to give us what we need. Just as Hannah asked for a baby and Hezekiah prayed for healing, we can bring our requests to God. He is able to do what we cannot. Pour out everything that is weighing on your heart today. Some days, all I can pray is, "Lord, I don't know what I need, but please help me." The Lord knows what you need. You don't have to speak articulate words or offer long prayers. Pray about anything and everything, and pray without ceasing (1 Thessalonians 5:17).

Jesus began this prayer focusing on our greatest hope: God's glory. He ended by focusing on our greatest problem: sin. This is a helpful reminder for us as parents, isn't it? My child's greatest problem isn't their friend group, their report card, or their screen time. Their biggest problem is their battle with sin and their need for forgiveness. It's our greatest need too.

Ourselves: A Good Heart Check

Prayer is a good heart check for us as parents: What do I need to confess? Have I been impatient? Unkind? Unloving? Taking the time to consider our own need for forgiveness each day will make us more tender-hearted toward others who need our forgiveness, especially our children. God's mercy and kindness toward our mistakes helps us to be patient and gracious toward our children in their mistakes. Prayer helps to reorient us and remind us of our own need for grace and forgiveness as we extend these blessings to our children.

Prayer also helps us to slow down and consider: Do I need to apologize to my teen for anything? Do I need to ask for their forgiveness? While our teens will make many mistakes, it's good to remember that we're not perfect either. By asking forgiveness from our teens, we model taking responsibility for our behavior and help them understand that we all need grace and forgiveness. Watching us apologize and own our mistakes teaches them how to do the same. As you pray, take the time to consider not just your teens' behavior, but your own.

We also want to pray that God will deliver our teens from evil. They face so many temptations: pride, coveting, sexual sin, lying, and peer pressure in a variety of forms. You may not know all the battles that are going on inside their heart. They may never share some of the struggles they are experiencing. But you can pray that God would deliver them, that he would protect them, that he would save them from the thief who "comes only to steal and kill and destroy" (John 10:10). God can help them to stand strong in the midst of the hurricane-force cultural winds that want to tear them apart.

Praying the Lord's prayer reorients our focus on God and reminds us that his will is best. It teaches us to seek God as Father and pour out all our requests before him. It also refocuses our prayers on the battle against sin—both for us and our teens. As you pray for your teens each day, I encourage you to begin with the Lord's prayer and use it as your guide.

Purposeful Parenting: Engaging Gracefully

We want to pray for our teens, and we hope to pray with them. The combination of both sets an example for them to follow. They see us relying on the Lord through prayer, and they learn to go to God in prayer themselves. My daughter wrote the foreword to my book *5 Things to Pray for Your Kids*. In it, she explained the impact of both:

> My mom once said prayer was like learning another language. If you grew up with parents who prayed regularly in the home, it would feel natural—like a native language you'd spoken since birth. But if you waited, it became harder to learn. It wasn't that you couldn't learn to pray, but it would take more time for it to feel natural. It might feel foreign or odd and somewhat uncomfortable at first.
>
> That's why I'm so grateful to have grown up with prayerful parents. From a young age, I was taught what prayer was and how to do it. I prayed with others at church, school, meals, and family devotions. It was always just a part of who I was and felt like a normal part of life. Looking back on the past seventeen years of learning and growing in prayer, I realize what an impact my parents praying for me and with me have had.
>
> My parents didn't give me a class to teach me how to pray. There was no instruction manual, video, or lecture. I simply learned by watching them pray each and every day. Every evening, sitting by my bed, my dad would read a Bible story and pray with my siblings and me. Every morning, I would come downstairs for school and see my mom finishing up her quiet time as she wrote out her prayers to the Lord. I knew that, among other things, she had been praying for me—asking God to grow my knowledge and love of Christ.
>
> And in a way, God used my mom's prayers to answer my mom's prayers: it was through seeing her alone with the Lord

every morning that I began to prioritize this same sort of time for myself and understand the importance of it.[3]

I've found that praying for and with others is one of the most loving and servant-hearted things we can do for them. Prayer builds a lifeline for our children that they can access whenever they are lonely, scared, hurting, or disappointed. It also gives them an opportunity to express thankfulness when they are rejoicing. Prayer is a form of intimacy with God that we get to teach our children. We cannot promise our children that we will always be with them. However, Romans 8:38-39 promises that "neither… height nor depth, nor anything else in all creation, will be able to separate us from the love of God in Christ Jesus our Lord." God will always be with our teens, even when we are not.

Prayer builds a lifeline for our children that they can access whenever they are lonely, scared, hurting, or disappointed.

As we seek to be prayerful parents, it's helpful to think about two general categories of prayer as we pray together with our teens: scheduled and spontaneous.

Scheduled Prayer Times

Creating a prayerful family takes thoughtfulness. It doesn't just happen. One of the best ways to teach our teens how to pray is to pray regularly with them. Scripture gives us guidance on what to pray for, and that can help us as we create routines in our home.

I mentioned in the previous chapter that our family regularly reads a passage of Scripture or a devotional each morning before school. We also pray together. To help us pray, I created cards with specific requests for each day—requests that come under four different headings:

- Pray for a member of our family
- Pray for a missionary we support
- Pray for leaders in our life (bosses, church leaders, government officials, principals)
- Pray for our neighbors, our world, and current events

Prayer for a Family Member

Our prayer cards rotate through a five-day cycle—which works well for us because we have five people in our family. If you have more or fewer family members, you could double up people per day or add extended family members to your cards, or use all seven days of the week.

We begin by asking the family member whose day it is, "How can we pray for you this week?" This simple check-in question is a positive way we find out about different concerns weighing on each of our teens' hearts. They often share about an upcoming test, a sporting event, or a friend who is going through a difficult time. We pray together for healing from colds and broken bones, as well as wisdom for choosing classes or colleges.

We have three additional categories on our cards: leaders, missionaries, and current events. Under the leader category, we rotate each day between pastors, bosses, school principals, and governing officials. Our missionary category rotates between the different missionaries we support—some local and some far away. And the current-events category rotates between personal, national, and world events that are happening (sick friends, natural disasters, and world conflicts).

We pray for these categories, seeking to follow these biblical principles:

Prayer for One Another

- "Rejoice in hope, be patient in tribulation, be constant in prayer" (Romans 12:12).

Prayer for Leaders

- "I urge that supplications, prayers, intercessions, and thanksgivings be made for all people, for kings and all who are in high positions, that we may lead a peaceful and quiet life, godly and dignified in every way" (1 Timothy 2:1-2).

Prayers for Missionaries and Their Work

- "Continue steadfastly in prayer, being watchful in it with thanksgiving. At the same time, pray also for us, that God may open to us a door for the word, to declare the mystery of Christ" (Colossians 4:2-3).
- "He said to them, 'The harvest is plentiful, but the laborers are few. Therefore pray earnestly to the Lord of the harvest to send out laborers into his harvest'" (Luke 10:2).

Prayers for Neighbors and World Events

- "Is anyone among you suffering? Let him pray. Is anyone cheerful? Let him sing praise. Is anyone among you sick? Let him call for the elders of the church, and let them pray over him, anointing him with oil in the name of the Lord" (James 5:13-14).
- "Kingship belongs to the Lord, and he rules over the nations" (Psalm 22:28).

Prayer is a powerful way to help our teens navigate the world around them. Multiple studies show that teens are suffering from heightened anxiety. While we don't know all the reasons, we do know we are living in an age of unprecedented access to information and world events. Daily, our teens are bombarded with news happening all around the globe, as well as next door. Like never before, they are able to see the suffering of people far away, and in the very next moment, see a picture of a party they weren't invited to.

It's a lot to handle.

Just like us, our teens are finite beings trying to process an infinite amount of information. Encouraging our children to pray is a way to help ease the burdens they are carrying each day. For them to learn to entrust current events, tests, illnesses, and friendships to the Lord allows them to experience his peace in the midst of hardship.

Prayer is a pathway to peace—it's a God-ordained way to find comfort in the midst of a world we can't control.

As Paul explained to the Philippians, "Do not be anxious about anything, but in everything by prayer and supplication with thanksgiving let your requests be made known to God. And the peace of God, which surpasses all understanding, will guard your hearts and your minds in Christ Jesus" (Philippians 4:6-7). Prayer is a pathway to peace—it's a God-ordained way to find comfort in the midst of a world we can't control. Our teens need to know how to pray, and they need to know they can pray at any time of the day.

Spontaneous Prayer

It's good to have planned times of prayer, but Scripture also invites us to pray without ceasing. We can pray wherever we are for whatever we need. And we can show our teens we love them by praying for and with them all throughout the day.

We all have rough days. And sometimes, our teens don't respond well. Often, the difficulties they encounter at school or with a friend are processed by grumpy moods, rolled eyes, and slammed doors. While it can be tempting to respond to every act of disrespect with a lecture or consequence of some sort, it's good for us as parents to take a moment and breathe deeply and pause to pray. Yes, perhaps your teen is taking everything bad in their life out on you. However, we're the adults. We have an opportunity to resist the temptation to respond to our teen's emotional outburst with one of our own. Pray and ask God to make you like him—slow to anger, abounding in love (Exodus 34:6).

Rather than meet your teen's grumpiness or disrespect with criticism or confrontation, begin by asking questions: "It seems like you're having a hard day. Did something happen at school?" "Did I do something to upset you?" Teens usually respond well to a kind word when they know they're acting poorly. They are dealing with all sorts of emotions that are hard to process at their age. Sometimes, I don't know why I'm grumpy at 50! They may not even know why they are upset, but you can always offer to pray for them and with them. It matters. It's a way to meet their difficult day with compassion and kindness.

Prayer is also a way to help teens as they prepare for the future or encounter unmet expectations. Many teens are worried about the future and they wonder: *Will I make the sports team or the play? Will I get asked to prom? Where will I go to college? Who will be my roommate?*

As adults, sometimes we discount the fears and uncertainties our teens are facing. We may casually brush aside their concerns as insignificant. Or, we may become overly worried about their concerns…and make them even more anxious because of our anxiety.

Rather than belittle their concerns or become overly anxious, turn to prayer with your teen. So many times, simply saying, "This situation seems difficult. I don't know what to do either. Can I pray for you?" is better than trying to have all the answers. Taking concerns before the Lord with your teen is a way you can actively care for them, teach them, and encourage them all at the same time.

Doing this might feel overly simplistic, but prayer matters. God uses our prayers and asks us to pray. Even though we might not always understand how prayer works, it does.

Practical Advice: Living Wisely

In the previous chapter, we talked about God's Word and teaching our children to love and obey it. We also discussed the different parenting styles: authoritarian, authoritative, and permissive. We'll close this chapter by considering the importance of bringing God's Word and prayer together as you develop your family's household rules.

It's tempting as Christian parents to take an authoritarian/domineering view of rules in the home. In this style of parenting, the basic premise is the parents make the rules and children obey them. While that may seem like a biblical approach, it's important to remember the following.

First, God is the only perfect parent. His rules are always right and good, perfectly ordained for his people. He made us and knows us. Because he is perfect, his commands for us are perfect. We want to encourage our children to love and obey God's Word. If God makes the rule, then we should do everything we can to encourage our children to obey God. Our household rules should always align with and support God's Word.

When it comes to creating additional household rules for our families, it's important to remember we aren't perfect. We may come up with rules that sound good in theory but don't really work in practice. Some rules may exasperate our teens because they are convenient for us as parents, but not age appropriate. Our word is not God's Word. We may get it wrong, so we need humility. Parenting biblically doesn't mean we force our teens to obey whatever rules we set based on our preferences or what everyone else in our community is doing. It means we are prayerful, considerate, and thoughtful as we create rules for our household. We want to create rules that bless and benefit our teens, protecting them from the negative influences of the world while allowing them to enjoy the good things God has created.

We also want to guard against permissive parenting. While some parents may be too strident in their rules, other parents can be too lax. Our teens need boundaries. It's right and good for us to establish household rules. Our teens are wise to listen to our advice and follow our instructions (Proverbs 13:1).

Both permissive and authoritarian parents tend to be driven by fear. Permissive parents fear that if they give rules or require accountability, their teens won't like them. Authoritarian parents tend to fear that if they give any freedom to their teens, they will lose control.

We want to guard against overly protective rules or a lack of rules altogether. To do so, we need to replace fear with faith as prayerful parents. Our goal is to create a warm, authoritative environment. Frankly, this is the most complicated type of parenting. It's much easier to make whatever rules you want (and try to keep control) or not have any rules at all. However, our teens need us to take the more difficult road. We can't just set the same rules as everyone else in our community. We need to do the hard work—the heart work—and prayerfully consider our parenting boundaries.

To do this, we need both the Word and prayer. We need wisdom from God as we parent our teens. God speaks to us in his Word, transforming our minds (Romans 12:2). We speak to God in prayer, asking him for divine guidance and wisdom (James 1:5).

It's much easier as parents to look for wisdom in a parenting book, a community of friends, or the latest and greatest new parenting techniques. None of those are bad places to seek advice (and I hope this book is helpful!). However, there are no easy answers. Everyone's situation is different, and we are all limited in the advice we can give. Only God knows our situation, and he knows it better than we do. That's why we go to him. We read the Bible and we pray. Daily. Consistently. Constantly. Parenting may feel a bit like wandering in the desert for 40 years, and you may feel like you don't know where you are going. God doesn't show us the whole plan, but he promises that his Word is a lamp to our feet and a light to our path (Psalm 119:105).

Practically, what does all this mean? It means that as parents, we give our teens boundaries. That is right and good. The boundaries in your home need to be considerate of each of your children. It's normal to have different rules for different children. A teen boy at 17 may have more freedoms than his 14-year-old sister. Yes, she will complain that it's not fair. That's okay.

It's also okay to scrap rules that you made early on and realize aren't working anymore for your family. Perhaps you hoped to have a "no dating until you're a certain age" type of rule. (Truthfully, I think every family who sets this rule tends to have teens who end up dating before the age they set.) The Bible doesn't set rules on dating ages, so typically this is a parental preference. That means *it's okay to change your mind.* You can reevaluate your rules as time goes on and make changes as needed based on what's best for your family. Don't let your pride get you stuck on a hill that's not worth dying on. Listen to your teens if they feel a rule you've made is too strident. Have the conversation. Listen to their perspective. Offer feedback—this is the age to invite your teens into the "whys" of your rules. It helps them gain discernment as they learn how to make their own choices and decisions.

Parenting teens would be a lot easier if there was a one-size-fits-all playbook for each age and stage. Instead, God invites you in this season of parenting to be dependent on him as you train your teen. You may feel lonely, unsure, and afraid, but he is right beside you. Just like my mom was there with me in Scotland teaching me how to bathe little Emma, God is your guide and will give you wisdom. He directs you in the Word, he guides you through prayer, and he leads you by his Spirit.

A Note of Gospel Hope

Prayer offers a special kind of intimacy. If you haven't prayed very often with your teens throughout their childhood, you may feel like it would be awkward to begin making prayer a routine. Or perhaps you felt comfortable when they were little, but you've fallen out of the habit of praying with them now that they're older.

Let me encourage you; It's never too late to begin. Prayer is one of our most powerful resources as parents. The Lord is available right now and welcomes you into his presence. Start by praying for your teens. The book of Hebrews instructs us, "Let us then with confidence draw near to the throne of grace, that we may receive mercy and find grace to help in time of need" (Hebrews 4:16). Jesus is able to sympathize with you and invites you to come with confidence. This is such good news!

You can also invite your teens to pray with you. If your teens don't want to pray out loud with you at this stage, that's okay. Sometimes they feel awkward about everything during these years, and they can be timid and unsure of what to say. You can offer to pray out loud for them. Your faithful prayers will teach them the language of prayer.

Just remember: God welcomes you and your prayers matter. The King of all the earth has the power. Seek him, trust him, and release your cares to him.

MK

Parenting Principles to Ponder

- Prayer is God's means of giving us wisdom and insight.
- Praying with our kids teaches them how to pray.
- Godly dependence frees us from controlling self-reliance as parents.

CHAPTER 3

Our Home Away from Home: The Church

Throughout my middle and high school years, the TV show *Cheers* was a popular fixture in American homes. The show centered on the interconnected stories of regular customers and employees at a local Boston bar. It ran for 11 seasons, aired 275 episodes, and earned 28 Emmy awards. I'm not sure if I can remember any other sitcom theme song, but I can easily recite the opening of *Cheers*. You could probably hum the tune along with me and be reminded of someplace in your life that's warm and welcoming, a little bit like home.

Cheers became a place where each of the characters felt known, understood, and loved. We can all relate, can't we? We all want someone to care about us, to listen to us as we share our struggles, to be glad to see us, and to know our name.

This desire to be known, to have someone to share life with, is as old as the Garden of Eden. The first "not good" in all of history happened before sin entered the picture. The Lord said, "It is not good that the man should be alone; I will make him a helper fit for him" (Genesis 2:18). Adam was created in the image of a triune, relational God. In the midst of a perfect world, Adam rightly had relational needs. We're not created to be alone. We need one another.

Our families provide the first sense of belonging that we have as young children. Extended family members can offer additional support, encouragement, and love. Neighborhoods help us find community outside of our family. Cities come together to celebrate sports teams, states and regions form our identities and accents, and countries offer shared languages and cultural behaviors. We want to be a part of something bigger than ourselves. We want to belong.

Tweens and teens are at a particularly difficult crossroads in their sense of belonging. They want to be unique individuals, and, at the same time, they desperately want to be a part of the crowd—whatever crowd that might be. Their peer relationships increase in importance but are full of instability. Best friends can move, new friendships can replace old friendships, activities can unite or divide, and new class schedules at middle and high schools can make a tween or teen feel like they are entering an entirely different school environment each year. It's a relational maze for adolescents to navigate.

As parents, it's important for us to understand that our kids need the stability of family, while also understanding that it's normal for kids at this age to want a larger sense of community. Many families seek to fill these needs through sports, activities, neighborhoods, and schools.

However, in the midst of trying to form healthy communities for our children, sometimes we neglect the community the Lord established for his people: the church.

While all believers are members of the larger, worldwide "invisible" church (all the people of God), it's important for believers to be part of a local congregation. We want our children to be a part of a community of faith, to know and be known by other people who love Jesus. It's tempting to neglect going to church or just choose to "watch from home" when it fits our schedules. However, church is much more than Sunday morning worship. It's not just a download of spiritual information. It's a family. It has blessings to offer that can support our children long after they leave our homes. The church also supports us as parents.

I know some of you have been hurt by the church. Let me be honest: I have too. Some of my deepest sorrows have been from people in the church. However, I keep going back. I know I need the church. And I know my church needs me. We belong to one another and God has gifted us to serve one another. In this chapter, we'll consider biblical principles about the church, how to engage with our children in the life of the church, and practical advice for being a part of the church community.

Principles for Parents: Thinking Biblically

One Sunday as I was busily putting the kids in the car to head to church, I looked up and noticed that all my neighbors were just starting their day. And no one else was thinking about going to church. One neighbor was out for a walk, one was picking up the newspaper in her robe, and one home looked like everyone was still fast asleep. We'd already been up for hours busily preparing to get everyone out the door. At that moment, I have to admit, I looked over the fence and the grass was looking greener at my neighbors' homes. I thought to myself, *How nice it would be to just stay in and have a slow morning.*

It can be tough to get to church, especially with children. We all have things we'd rather do: sleep in, vacation, participate in travel sports teams, go for a walk, read the paper, or make a big breakfast together as a family. And those can be good things. However, if they replace our church attendance as a family, they will interfere with an important part of our own spiritual development, as well as the spiritual development of our children.

It's helpful to begin this chapter by considering these questions: Do we need to go to church? Does it really make a difference in our spiritual lives? Wouldn't it be just as good to sit at home and listen to a "better" sermon from a pastor across the country than join and be part of a local congregation? I want us to begin thinking through those questions by considering five important ways the church benefits us: it's a place for worship, learning, care, service, and belonging.

A Place to Worship

Hebrews explains the privilege we have as Christians in approaching God. Consider these words:

> Let us draw near with a true heart in full assurance of faith, with our hearts sprinkled clean from an evil conscience and our bodies washed with pure water. Let us hold fast the confession of our hope without wavering, for he who promised is faithful. And let us consider how to stir up one another to love and good works, not neglecting to meet together, as is the habit of some, but encouraging one another, and all the more as you see the Day drawing near (Hebrews 10:22-25).

The Old Testament saints had many regulations for their worship, and the book of Leviticus explains all the various ways people could be declared unclean and separated from temple worship. In contrast, we can draw near, knowing that Christ has cleansed our hearts completely. We have full access. It's a privilege to be able to draw near to God with other believers.

This passage also warns us not to neglect meeting together. Our faith is not simply a personal belief system. It's part of a corporate, familial experience. We pray to "our Father" as we live in community together. It's a corporate "let us draw near" rather than an individual drawing near. There's something about gathering together to worship God that strengthens our faith. Doing this is important, and we are commanded to continue to meet together, encouraging one another as we do.

As we parent teens, it matters that we go to church. It's important for them to understand that faith is more than personal. We are giving them the opportunity to learn how to worship God: to pray, to hear from his

Word, to participate in the Lord's supper, and to sing praises to his name. We're teaching them that worshipping God is a corporate affair.

A Place for Learning

Church also offers opportunities for growth as we learn about faith from other believers. Paul's letter to the Ephesians explains:

> He gave the apostles, the prophets, the evangelists, the shepherds and teachers, to equip the saints for the work of ministry, for building up the body of Christ, until we all attain to the unity of the faith and of the knowledge of the Son of God, to mature manhood, to the measure of the stature of the fullness of Christ, so that we may no longer be children (Ephesians 4:11-16).

Just as worship is a corporate experience, spiritual growth also happens within community. If we want a sturdy faith that can withstand cultural changes and influences, we need the nourishment of the church. We're all part of one another and dependent upon one another for growth. We need equipping, and God has given shepherds and teachers for the purpose of building up the church.

While it may seem like your teens aren't listening to anything being said in the sermon or Sunday school, they are probably taking in more than you realize. God's Word goes out in the church, and he promises that it won't return void (Isaiah 55:11). We may not see the fruit right away, but over time, the lessons learned within the community of the church are able to strengthen our teens so that they grow more mature in the faith.

As parents, we also need the equipping the church provides. We never graduate from learning the truths of the gospel. Whether we are 15 or 50, we need the fortifying nourishment that the church offers. The preached Word offers strength for the weary, comfort for the hurting, guidance for the lost, and courage for the fearful. The church is God's means of equipping you for your tasks as a believer.

We never graduate from learning the truths of the gospel.

A Place for Care

The church offers a place for worship and teaching, as well as a place for shepherding care. Peter exhorted the elders of the church, "Shepherd the flock of God that is among you, exercising oversight, not under compulsion, but willingly, as God would have you; not for shameful gain, but eagerly; not domineering over those in your charge, but being examples to the flock" (1 Peter 5:2-3).

We all need guidance. Sheep tend to go astray. They need a shepherd to go after them and show them the way back to the path. We also need instruction. When you feel unsure of how to parent your teen, the advice of an older believer in the church may help you in tremendous ways. A 70-year-old mom can offer you wisdom and guidance gained through years of experience. A 24-year-old in your congregation might be able to interact with and encourage your teen when they aren't willing to listen to you. The elders serve as examples to follow and care for the church with their faithful prayers and service. Being part of a church provides a wealth of resources for you and your family—it's a blessing to put yourself in a place that you and your teen can grow together.

A Place for Service

The church is not just a place we go to so we can grow and be cared for, it is a place that we serve one another in love. Every believer has spiritual gifts that are to be used in community, as 1 Corinthians 12:4-7 teaches:

> Now there are varieties of gifts, but the same Spirit; and there are varieties of service, but the same Lord; and there are varieties

of activities, but it is the same God who empowers them all in everyone. To each is given the manifestation of the Spirit for the common good.

As your children see you using your gifts within the church, they will learn that the church isn't just about the work of the pastor and the other leaders. Every member matters. In fact, teens matter! They have something to give too.

Sometimes, we attempt to make church appeal to teens by trying to make everything entertaining for them. However, when they are equipped and expected to use their gifts to serve in the church, they actually feel more connected to the body. It's not a burden, but a blessing for our teens to serve. Whether it's visiting with an elderly member, helping to clean up after an event, taking part in singing or the worship music, passing out the bulletins, or serving in the church nursery, encourage your teens to serve in the church. Over time, they will build relationships as they serve. Teens grow in confidence as they use the unique gifts God has given them to be a blessing to others.

A Place to Belong

My pinky finger works only when connected to my hand. My hand needs my arm. My arm needs my shoulder. All these parts belong to my body, even though they are individual members with specific functions. The church works the same way. As 1 Corinthians 12:26-27 reminds us, "If one member suffers, all suffer together; if one member is honored, all rejoice together. Now you are the body of Christ and individually members of it."

As we discussed at the beginning of this chapter, we're created for community. We sometimes think of marriage as the ultimate community. However, earthly marriages point to a bigger and better marriage that is yet to come, the wedding supper of the Lamb and his bride, the church (Revelation 19:7-9). The church is our community here on earth while we long for our home in heaven.

Teens desperately want to belong. They may search for that sense of belonging in all the wrong places, but the longing is a good one. In just a few years, your teens will be on their own. They may choose to stay in your city, or they may move far away. The church is able to provide a "home away from home" wherever they go. We're meant to be a large extended family— brothers, sisters, mothers, fathers, sons, and daughters. My daughter Emma explained the importance of church for her when she went to college:

> Church felt like a normal part of my life from a young age, but attending college has strengthened my love for the local church. It's been a home away from home. When my housemates and I were quarantined, my church brought us food. Church members have welcomed us into their homes. Elders have prayed over me and helped answer difficult questions. Pastors have exhorted us to go make disciples.[1]

As parents, we cannot always be there for our children. One day, they will go off into the world. One of the best gifts we can give them is letting church be a normal part of their lives so they feel comfortable going to church. This matters more than we may realize. Studies show that parents who are consistent in their church engagement (without being overbearing) are most effective in passing on their beliefs to the next generation.[2] Demonstrating everyday faithfulness in our own lives communicates healthy spiritual habits to our children.

The church is a source of rich blessings for ourselves and our children. Yes, we may want the ease of a Sunday morning spent in bed, but we need the church. We have a place to worship God, grow in faith, receive care, use our gifts, and find true community and belonging. Don't neglect the body. You need the church, and so do your teens.

Purposeful Parenting: Engaging Gracefully

Faithfully attending church from a young age builds a pattern into our teens' lives. Hopefully, they can't imagine it being Sunday and not going to church. Just as surely as they know Chick-fil-A will be closed on Sunday, they expect to be in church on Sunday.

However, some teens will start to resist attending church as they reach adolescence. That brings up an important question: *What do I do when my teen doesn't want to go to church?*

If we think back to our three styles of parenting, there are two pitfalls to avoid: being overly permissive or authoritarian about church attendance. The permissive parent doesn't want to make their child do anything they don't want to do. So, if a child loses interest in church for some reason, the permissive parent will make excuses for their teen to avoid attending church. They can even seem like legitimate reasons: they needed more sleep, they had homework to do, or they would lose their spot on their sports team.

We may also struggle with the fear that "forcing" our children to attend church would be legalistic, or perhaps would make them bitter about Christianity in some way. However, we require our kids to do a lot of things they may not like to do. Perhaps your kids loved broccoli the first time they ate it, but mine sure didn't. It took a lot of telling my kids to eat their vegetables before they began enjoying them. And sometimes they still don't. But our kids need vitamins, so loving parents make their kids eat vegetables. Church is a vital part of our kids' spiritual health. Just like vegetables give needed physical nutrients, the church provides needed spiritual nourishment.

Currently, teens are facing an epidemic of loneliness. According to one study, "In a sample of one million adolescents, school loneliness increased between 2012 and 2018 in 36 out of 37 countries around the world. Nearly twice as many adolescents displayed high levels of loneliness in 2018 compared to 2012, an increase similar to that previously identified in clinical-level depression in the U.S. and UK."[3] Kids are more connected than ever, but lonelier than ever too. Many attribute this change to the use of cell phones and its adverse effects on teen social behavior.

According to *The Atlantic*, "The United States is experiencing an extreme teenage mental-health crisis. From 2009 to 2021, the share of American high-school students who say they feel 'persistent feelings of sadness or hopelessness' rose from 26 percent to 44 percent, according to a new CDC study. This is the highest level of teenage sadness ever recorded."[4]

Okay, so that's the bad news. However, there is good news. According to multiple studies, weekly church attendance makes a significant difference in teens' lives. Researchers reported:

> Participating in spiritual practices during childhood and adolescence may be a protective factor for a range of health and well-being outcomes in early adulthood, according to a new study from Harvard T.H. Chan School of Public Health. Researchers found that people who attended weekly religious services or practiced daily prayer or meditation in their youth reported greater life satisfaction and positivity in their 20s—and were less likely to subsequently have depressive symptoms, smoke, use illicit drugs, or have a sexually transmitted infection—than people raised with less regular spiritual habits.[5]

So, while it might be tempting to think we are loving our teens by letting them miss church, we're actually keeping them from something that is life-giving. And the benefits of church continue throughout young adulthood: "The results showed that people who attended religious services at least weekly in childhood and adolescence were approximately 18% more likely to report higher happiness as young adults (ages 23-30) than those who never attended services."[6]

The Bible and common-grace insights from research studies concur: Church is vital. It's a blessing to your teens, even when they don't feel like it or don't want to go.

On the other hand, we also don't want to fall into the trap of being authoritarian and overly rigid as we discuss church attendance with our teens. It's clear in Scripture that we're to have a habit of regularly meeting with the saints of God. That doesn't mean that we can never, under any circumstance, miss church. It also doesn't mean that our teens have to go to the church we attend (we'll discuss this more at the end of the chapter). I would caution against taking the "It's my way or the highway" approach with teens and church. Instead, I would encourage you to *have a conversation.*

As we seek to parent authoritatively (as shepherds), that means we do so with necessary guidelines, as well as with warmth in our communication. It's good to have established family rules like "We go to church every week." It's also good to carefully listen to your teen when they start complaining about going to church. Rather than give them all the reasons they need to be in church, or anxiously fretting about the state of their spiritual life, begin by asking some questions. Start with the simplest one: "Why don't you want to go?"

 **Understanding our teen's perspective is a vital part of creating a warm environment where faith (and questions about faith) can flourish.**

There are a few replies you may get to this question, and it's good to be mentally prepared to answer with some well-thought-out responses. However, if you're not sure how to respond or you don't have an answer, keep asking more questions. Understanding our teen's perspective is a vital part of creating a warm environment where faith (and questions about faith) can flourish. It's normal for teens, at their age, to differ from their parents as they try to figure out what they believe for themselves. Asking questions allows them to feel listened to and understood, even if you disagree.

There are a few common replies to the question, "Why don't you want to go?" Let's consider them.

"Church is boring"

For a variety of reasons, teens are frequently bored. It's not really a surprise that they would be bored with church sometimes. And, honestly, sometimes I'm bored in church too (not that I want to be!). Now isn't the time to try to convince your teen that church isn't boring—you probably won't win that battle. Instead, it's time to dig in a little deeper. Ask them which part of the service is most difficult. Ask them why they think it's boring. Also, tell them about your own struggles. If you find the singing repetitive or the sermons a bit long, or your mind wandering during the prayers, it's okay to share that with your teen. In fact, it may help them to know that you don't find every moment of the church service exciting.

It also helps to be sympathetic. Our kids spend every day in school learning. They don't get many mental breaks. Try to find ways to help them engage with the service. Ask them if there's a better place to sit or if it would help to have a pen and paper to take notes or doodle (this actually helps with focus and retention) during the sermon. Seek to find ways to help them engage as much as possible. It's also good to remind them that church is a priority. It is still necessary for them to go to school even when they're bored by it, so it's completely reasonable to tell them they still have to go to church.

"I don't know anyone"

Sometimes we feel alone, even in a crowd. Church can be intimidating for kids, especially if they feel like everyone else knows one another. Again, take the time to listen and ask more questions.

It's also helpful to consider ways that you can introduce your teen to others in the church in smaller settings. You could have another family with teens over for dinner. Or perhaps some young adults, just a stage or two ahead of your teen age-wise. Relationships with older mentors in their twenties can be so impactful for middle and high school-age kids.

As I look back, I realize that having church people in our home on a regular basis helped my children to feel a part of the community. We had people from all different life stages at our home for Bible studies, church social events, and various meetings throughout the years. Seeing people in our home and then on Sunday morning allowed our kids to know a variety of people, not just kids their own age. This familiarity can foster a sense of belonging that helps your teen feel at home in church.

It's also a good idea to ask your teen if they have friends who go to another church. If there aren't many teens at your church, perhaps they could attend the youth group at another church. Whatever you can do to foster those relationships (even if it means a lot of driving) will be a support to your teen.

"Everyone there is so judgmental"

It is during adolescence that our teens may start feeling the weight of their wrong choices, particularly in church. The Word of God "is living and active, sharper than any two-edged sword, piercing to the division of soul and of spirit, of joints and of marrow, and discerning the thoughts and intentions of the heart. And no creature is hidden from his sight, but all are naked and exposed to the eyes of him to whom we must give account" (Hebrews 4:12-13).

Conviction from God's Word may make our tweens and teens feel uncomfortable. And, truthfully, in our culture today, we don't talk a lot about guilt because we want people to feel accepted. However, God's Word exposes us to the reality of our sin. While this may not feel good, it's a grace to us (and our teens!). When we understand that we have a sin problem, we can begin to understand the good news of the sin solution: Jesus.

When we understand that we have a sin problem, we can begin to understand the good news of the sin solution: Jesus.

If your kids are feeling like everyone at church is judgmental, ask them what they mean by that. Dig deeper and ask if it's a particular person or Christian beliefs in general that they find judgmental. It's good to remind them that just because one person has a particular viewpoint doesn't mean that's the way everyone else in the church is thinking. It also helps to remind them that churches are full of different types of people with different perspectives on a variety of issues. It's a good lesson toward learning how to discern between primary issues of the faith and secondary issues on which we can agree to disagree (Romans 14).

"I don't believe any of this stuff"

A lack of belief is probably the most difficult reply for us to hear as parents. We want our teens to believe in Jesus. We've taught them, prayed for them, and hoped to be an example of faithful living. When we hear our teens say they have doubts, it's easy to immediately spiral into a pit of despair, wondering, *What did I do wrong?*

Let me give you a few words of encouragement. Many teenagers go through a season of doubt or distrust about the Bible or Christianity. Many of them come back to faith, and it's a faith that's stronger and more assured on the other side of their doubts.

So, when your teen says, "I don't believe any of this stuff," my best parenting advice is this: Be calm and carry on. I don't mean that in a trite way. Sometimes teens say things like this to unsettle us. They test boundaries and they push back, and they argue and sometimes they attack with laser precision the things we care about most. It's not about you. It's about them trying to figure out how to navigate their thoughts, emotions, and opinions. Yes, it is scary and concerning when that happens. However, you are never going to be able to convince your child to believe. Only the Spirit can do that.

I would encourage you to talk to them about their doubts. Ask good questions and listen well. Being calm when they are struggling is one of the best ways to allow them the freedom to ask questions about their faith. It's better for them to openly question Christianity with you than secretly doubt in silence. It's also good to help understand the nature of their doubts so that you can find resources that might encourage them.[7]

In these conversations, you don't need to have all the answers. Spend a lot of time listening. Don't squelch their willingness to talk to you by responding with dismissive arguments. Dig into the questions with them. Share your own doubts and struggles. And share how, in the midst of them, you came to be a person of faith.

Many strong believers I know (including the ones who speak on big stages and have many followers) have shared with me about their deep and painful seasons of doubt. It's a part of a growing faith that is sometimes scary to talk about. Walk with your child in the struggle, let them know you care, and be available. But see it as a struggle for faith, not as a rejection of you.

And, while they are struggling with doubts, invite them to take their concerns to a pastor or church leader. Church is a welcome place for seekers and doubters, as well as believers. Sermons can have a powerful impact on our teens. In the meantime, keep having honest conversations, keep listening, and keep praying. The Spirit can open their eyes to the truths of the Bible and the Word is able to make them wise for salvation (2 Timothy 3:15).

Practical Advice: Living Wisely

There's so much to consider when we talk about church and our teens. We'll close this chapter with a grab bag of practical topics to consider as you think about your church situation.

Church Culture

Every church has a unique culture, especially when it comes to the matter of parenting. There are many opinions about how to raise children, starting from the foods you eat while you're pregnant, to sleep training, to making sure to pick the best toys and books for brain development. These opinions often become more emotionally charged when it comes to topics like schooling, dating, cell phones, and clothing choices for teens. There can be a lot of pressure to make parenting decisions that align with the opinions of others in your church community.

However, each person has unique circumstances. One family may be able to afford a private Christian school. Another family may be struggling to make ends meet and their only option is public school. One woman may love homeschooling her children, while that might not be an option for another mom because of her work schedule. Each family has to prayerfully make their own decisions based on their circumstances, and not simply follow the expectations of others in their church community.

It can be difficult to make a parenting choice that differs from the choices of others who are in the same parenting stage as you. That's why I'm always so thankful for the community of the church and the ability to reach out to families who are just a stage or two beyond the teen years. Glean insights from their experience. Ask them what decisions they regret and what decisions they are thankful they made.

When I was in my first year of teaching, my mom (who was also a teacher) gave me wise advice. She told me, "When you have questions about teaching or if something is going wrong, it will be tempting to talk with the other younger teachers who may be having the same struggles so you can commiserate together. Instead of asking them for advice, find an older teacher who seems to manage her class with ease and ask her for advice. She's doing something that makes her class run differently—most likely small but impactful routines that benefit everyone in the classroom."

In a similar way, it's tempting for us as parents to look for advice from others who are in our exact same parenting stage or struggling with the same parenting issues. It's possible we may truly benefit from being able to discuss certain topics with others who are in or have been in the same situation (particularly with mental health struggles, learning disabilities, adoption issues, and other specific types of concerns). However, for general parenting advice, look to families who are a stage or two ahead of you and whose members enjoy being around one another. Ask them what they did to create a warm and loving environment in their home.

The church family can be a source of blessing as we parent our teens. I encourage you to lean on them for support. It's also good to be aware of and evaluate the culture of your church. Some churches have tendencies toward legalism. They may expect all parents to make choices that are not commanded in Scripture. And while those choices may work for some families or individual children, they might not be the wisest course of action for every family. That's why it is so important for us to be in the Word and praying, so that we can make the wisest decisions for each of our children.

There is no one way to parent. Be gracious with others when they make different decisions than you do. Another person's parenting decision is not an indictment or judgment of your parenting. There are wise, biblical principles we can glean from others, but there's no easy road map. As we make specific decisions, we must remain on our knees before the Lord, asking for wisdom and guidance. The church family works in conjunction with our time in the Word and prayer to form the foundation of our parenting. It's like a three-legged stool, with each leg having an important role in keeping the stool from falling over.

Changing Churches

One question that often arises during the tween and teen years is, Should I change churches for my teen? That's such a tough question to answer in a book because there are good reasons and less-than-good reasons to change churches. It would be much better if we were able to sit with a cup of coffee talking it over and weighing the pros and cons—which I encourage you to do with someone you trust as a mentor.

However, there are a few principles to consider as you attempt to answer this question. If you have come to realize the culture of your church is unhealthy or overly legalistic or rigid, it might be wise to consider attending a different church. We were once in a difficult situation that made leaving our church the only healthy option for our family. However, it was so painful to leave people we had loved and who had loved our children since they were born. This happened during their teen years, and I would have done anything I could have to avoid making that change during that season. But sometimes changes are necessary because of a church culture that is unhealthy.

In most instances, I would encourage you to stay in the church you've called your home. It's a blessing for teens to grow up around people who have known them since they were in the nursery. If your church doesn't have many teenagers, most larger churches are very welcoming to teens from other churches participating in their youth group activities. Be prayerful and thoughtful as you foster your teen's engagement in the church.

If an older teen (who can drive) would rather attend a different church, it's good to have an honest conversation about it and allow them to make their own choices. Our college-age daughter rarely attends church with us when she is home because she goes to another one in town. We are so thankful she's found a healthy church and is making wise spiritual choices on her own. While we'd all love to be in church together as a family, our goal is simply that our children be in church, hearing the Word preached and fellowshipping with other believers. It's good to keep this main goal in mind and be willing to let go of personal preferences when it comes to the churches our children choose to attend.

Church on Vacation

I know it's tough to think about going to church when you're on vacation, but I would encourage you to try it! When you're in another city, you have a wonderful opportunity for your family to be exposed to churches that are different than yours. One year at Easter, we were vacationing at the beach and found a wonderful church. That Sunday, they were having fully immersive baptisms, and my kids were fascinated. I realized they had never seen anything other than our church's practice of sprinkling for baptism. We talked about this afterward, and they had tons of baptism questions just because they had visited a different church. Attending other churches gives you an opportunity to discuss the beliefs and practices of various denominations. Such exposure can be a huge benefit before your kids go off to college so that they feel comfortable in a variety of church settings.

If you're traveling for vacation or sports reasons, I encourage you to visit The Gospel Coalition's church directory (https://www.thegospelcoalition.org/churches/). Put in a zip code and a list of Bible-believing churches will appear. By no means will the list be complete, but you might find this a helpful resource when you travel to another city.

Sabbath Rest

One final consideration about regular church attendance as a family is that it creates a rhythm of Sabbath rest in the home. In Exodus 20:8, God commanded the Israelites, "Remember the Sabbath day, to keep it holy." Jesus attended the synagogue regularly on the Sabbath (Luke 4:16). Paul went to the synagogue each week on the Sabbath to teach about Jesus as the fulfillment of the law and prophets (Acts 18:4). Even at the time of creation, we read that God rested on the seventh day (Genesis 2:2). As Christians, we observe the Sabbath on Sunday—which the New Testament refers to as the Lord's Day (Revelation 1:10) because Christ rose on that day.

Sunday is an opportunity to rest from our usual activities and spend time worshipping God, fellowshipping with others, and slowing down to enjoy the world God created.

After the days of creation, God rested as an example to us. Our lives are increasingly packed to the full, which leads to stress and anxiety, worry and exhaustion. Our children need to see us setting aside the Sabbath so that they can learn to spend one day a week focusing on the Lord and his people. Sabbath rest is a gift to us. We need rest. Our kids need rest.

Sunday is an opportunity to rest from our usual activities and spend time worshipping God, fellowshipping with others, and slowing down to enjoy the world God created. It's a day to set aside your everyday activities and invite a family from church over for a meal or to take an extended time to read a good book or meditate on the Bible. You have permission to take a day off each week and spend it with God—what a gift!

God's Word, prayer, and the church set a healthy foundation for us as parents. They're the basic building blocks for every Christian home. In the next few chapters, we'll consider the battles we face as parents. The topics we consider may surprise you. It's less about battling negative influences in culture or our teen's bad behavior, and more about looking inward and battling the idols that tempt us as parents. Thankfully, we'll also see that God's grace is sufficient in all things—even for parents.

A Note of Gospel Hope

I know finding a good church community and making church a priority with your teens isn't always easy. While regular church attendance may feel uncomfortable at first, eventually, it will feel like a normal (and welcome!) part of your family life. Even if you've struggled to be involved in the past or had negative experiences, I encourage you to try again.

Over the years, I've formed so many dear friendships through fellowship at church. These friends have welcomed me into their homes, loved on my kids, brought me meals when I was sick, and shared life with me. I've done the same for them. We've studied the Bible together, prayed together, cried together, and celebrated together. Life is better in the church. We bless our teens with a special community when we make church a regular routine of our family life.

MK

Parenting Principles to Ponder

- Church is an important part of spiritual growth and development for every member of the family.

- Church is a healthy place for teens to experience community and belonging.

- Listen to your teens' concerns about church. Have conversations and keep the communication lines open.

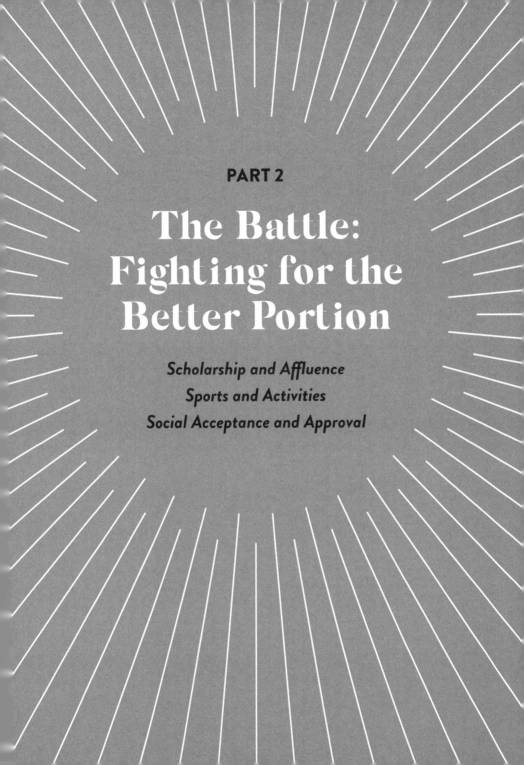

PART 2

The Battle: Fighting for the Better Portion

Scholarship and Affluence
Sports and Activities
Social Acceptance and Approval

Introduction

In the first section of this book, we considered the basic foundations of a Christian home—the Word, prayer, and the church. In the next few chapters, we'll turn our attention to the battle before us. You may think this is the section where we'll talk about the downward spiral of culture and cover topics like sex, drugs, and rock 'n' roll. Or perhaps we'll consider how to win the various battles with your tween over cell phones, homework assignments, and curfews.

Well, we're actually going to cover a more difficult topic: idolatry. And, not the kinds our kids deal with, but the ones lurking around our own hearts as parents. We'll consider the cultural idols that influence us, but our primary focus will be our own idols and how they negatively impact our parenting. We may be tempted to look outside of ourselves to find some magical elixir to solve all our parenting dilemmas, but the Bible directs us time and time again to the problem of idolatry and the damage that follows.

As we begin this section, you may find yourself wondering what I mean by idolatry. Many people think of idolatry in terms of carved images and statues that ancient people worshipped. The Bible does warn against this type of idolatry. The second commandment says, "You shall not make for yourself a carved image, or any likeness of anything that is in heaven above, or that is in the earth beneath, or that is in the water under the earth. You shall not bow down to them or serve them" (Exodus 20:4-5).

Other verses speak to the foolishness of trusting in something made by human hands: "What profit is an idol when its maker has shaped it, a metal image, a teacher of lies? For its maker trusts in his own creation when he makes speechless idols! Woe to him who says to a wooden thing, Awake; to a silent stone, Arise! Can this teach? Behold, it is overlaid with gold and silver, and there is no breath at all in it" (Habakkuk 2:18-19).

In contrast to these speechless and breathless idols, God speaks and life bursts forth—Adam was only dust from the ground until God breathed life into him (Genesis 2:7). Created idols have no breath, so they can never be life-giving. Most of us can see the worthlessness of trusting in an object of stone or wood. How can a created thing give us security? Why would people bow down and worship something made by human hands? It doesn't make much sense to our modern minds.

Well, if our problem were merely carved images and statues, we could all easily remove them from our homes and lives. However, the idolatry Scripture warns against is not limited to created statues. It's a much bigger problem than we might imagine. In his book *Counterfeit Gods*, Tim Keller offers this definition:

> What is an idol? It is anything more important to you than God, anything that absorbs your heart and imagination more than God, anything you seek to give you what only God can give. A counterfeit god is anything so central and essential to your life that, should you lose it, your life would feel hardly worth living. An idol has such a controlling position in your heart that you can spend most of your passion and energy, your emotional and financial resources, on it without a second thought.[1]

An idol can be anything we love more than God. It can be anything we trust in for ultimate fulfillment. It can be where we put our joy, expectations, and security. Usually, they aren't bad things in and of themselves. Often they are good gifts that we cling to in such a way that they become our ultimate hope, even more than God.

This means that anything in our life can become an idol. Whether it's our jobs, our homes, our children, money, appearance, health, or ministry—whatever we seek, serve, and love in place of God is an idol in our heart. There are infinite ways we can fall into the trap of idolatry. It's why the sixteenth-century theologian John Calvin once said, "The human mind is, so to speak, a perpetual forge of idols."[2] This problematic reality is what makes idolatry such a battlefield in our role as parents.

Source Idols

We also have layers of idolatry—there are idols beneath our idols. We have both *source* idols and *surface* idols (some people call these root and fruit idols). Source idols are the motivating factors underneath the idols that rise to the surface. Tim Keller refers to source idols as "deep" idols and explains the four most common ones: "Each deep idol—power, approval, comfort, or control—generates a different set of fears and a different set of hopes."[3] Each of these four source idols has different motivations, emotions, and fears. From the following descriptions, consider which source idols you tend to struggle with the most (and it's possible to have more than one):

The source idol of *power* is usually at the core of a person who is driven by success, influence, recognition, or supremacy. They will usually be competitive and confident, while struggling with emotions of anger and frustration. They are willing to be overburdened with responsibility, and their core fear is humiliation.[4]

The source idol of *approval* is usually at the core of a person who is driven by a desire for love, affirmation, acceptance, and connection. They will usually be likeable, while struggling with emotions of fear and cowardice. Their core fear is rejection, and they may be overly sensitive or insecure in relationships.

The source idol of *comfort* is usually at the core of a person who is driven by a desire for ease, pleasure, and a lack of stress. They will usually be easygoing and less productive while struggling with feelings of boredom. Their core fears are stress and demands, which can lead to others feeling hurt or neglected.

The source idol of *control* is usually at the core of a person who is driven by rules, routines, and everything going according to their plan. They will usually be competent and individualistic, while struggling with feelings of anxiety. They may experience loneliness, and their core fears are uncertainty, unpredictable circumstances, and unreliable people.

Surface Idols

In addition to source idols, we have plenty of other idols that spring up to the surface of our lives. Surface idols can include appearance, work, money, family, friendships, school choices, social status, materialism, health, ideology, ministry, and a variety of other things that we rely on for our significance and value.

Surface idols are usually easier to spot (especially in other people!). We can observe a dad's obsession with sports that is negatively affecting his son. We can see a mom who idolizes health and ideal weight being overzealous about the dangers of food additives and the benefits of organic and free-range farms. We can notice a dad who idolizes money spending all his time working so he can get a larger bonus each year.

While we can recognize such idols in others, it may take some thoughtful time of reflection to spot surface idols in our own life. It's good to be on the lookout for them. Take a few moments to reflect upon the following questions, which can help you identify various surface idols in your life.

Questions to Consider

Who/what do you fear losing? Who/what do you love?

Love and fear tend to go hand and hand. Whomever we love deeply, we will fear losing. And it's good to love people, places, and even things—God created a world full of wonder that we are invited to enjoy. However, because of sin, our love can become idolatrous. Rather than trust in God, we grow anxious and controlling in our fear. Consider what you most fear losing, and how you tend to deal with those fears.

What do you spend your time, money, and thoughts on?

We all have limited resources. Some people have a lot of time, but little money. Others have lots of money and little time. Our idols often surface in connection with what we're spending our time and money on. Some people will use these resources for entertainment or acceptance. Others will use their time and money to secure power or influence.

All of us have only so much we can think about during the day. Where does your mind tend to wander? What do you dream about? What worries you? What do you think about when you're not really thinking?

What do you trust in for security or comfort? What do you hope in?

When you've had a bad day, what is your go-to for comfort? Perhaps when you are anxious, you respond by checking your bank account, scrolling through social media likes, or going shopping for a new outfit. Wherever we turn when our days get difficult, or we feel weary, often exposes idols in our lives.

What do you want that others have? What do you respect in others?

Picture someone in your life whom you respect. Why do look up to them? What do they have that you long for? What we admire in others is often a sign of what we value or find significant. It's also helpful to consider how you would answer the question, What would make me successful in life?

Asking yourself these questions is helpful because if you want to battle your idols, it starts with understanding where you turn for your sense of security. While it may seem more reasonable or even harmless to trust in money or appearance or health, these things are no more able to truly help us than idols crafted of wood and stone.

Source and Surface Idols Together

It's helpful to understand that the four source idols—power, approval, comfort, and control—can sometimes appear similar on the surface. For instance, many people have the same surface idolatry of money. For the person whose source idol is power, they may long for money because it puts them in positions of leadership in organizations and with people. For another person, they may have a surface idolatry of money, but their source idol is comfort. Money is the conduit by which they can have the comforts they desire. One person may idolize money because having the ability to purchase beautiful things gives them social approval. Another person may idolize money because it makes them feel in control of their life circumstances. Therefore, we may have the same surface idol as our neighbor, but the reason behind our desire for money, friendship, appearance, or work might be very different.

Like weeds in our garden, these source idols can grow in all sorts of ways and spring up to the surface in every place imaginable—especially our parenting. If we think back to our three types of parenting—permissive, authoritative, and authoritarian—different idols are at the root of the two most problematic parenting styles.

Permissive parents are most likely driven by the source idols of approval and comfort, while *authoritarian parents* are most likely driven by the source idols of power and control.

Cultural Idols

In addition to source (power, approval, control, comfort) idols and surface idols, there are cultural idols that we need to be aware of as we parent our teens. Think about it this way: Source idols are the soil from which our surface idols spring up like weeds. Cultural idols are like a contaminated river that's flowing through our backyard (and our neighbors'). The groundwater contamination is affecting the soil and producing similar surface idols among groups of people. This cultural contamination can make certain forms of idolatry seem "normal" because of the collective effect.

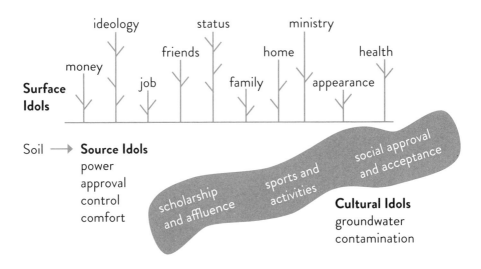

Warning for Parents

Source, surface, and cultural idols affect our parenting in various ways. Each parent brings their own set of idols into the home (between my husband and me, I think we have all four source idols covered!). It's like unwanted junk spilling out of all our drawers and cabinets.

And it doesn't just make a mess in our own lives—our idolatry greatly affects our children. One Bible verse that has always convicted me is 2 Kings 17:41:

> Even while these people were worshiping the LORD, *they were serving their idols.* To this day their children and grandchildren continue to do as their ancestors did (NIV, emphasis added).

In the midst of "worshiping the LORD," the people were ultimately serving their idols. They were religious, but their affections were displaced from the Lord and wrongly focused on their idols.

And guess what happened? (I hate this part.)

Their children and grandchildren did just what their parents were doing— they served the same idols rather than serving God.

Our kids are not only negatively impacted by the fruit of idolatry (which inevitably will spring up toward them in impatience, unkindness, or anger), they will end up following us right into the same miserable pit.

This is a warning to us all. We can be fastidious about attending church, reading our Bibles, and saying our prayers—worshipping the Lord—while still serving our idols. The Christian life is a combination of putting *on* good things and putting *off* bad things. The apostle Paul tells us to put on the new self, which is being renewed in knowledge after the image of our creator, while at the same time putting to death everything in us that is earthly: "sexual immorality, impurity, passion, evil desire, and covetousness, which is idolatry" (Colossians 3:5).

As parents, we're building our homes on the basic foundations of the Bible, prayer, and the church (that's what we're putting on each day), while at the same time doing battle with the idolatry that lurks in our hearts (that's what we're putting off). God calls us to build our lives on his truth and, at the same time, to clear out the dirt of sin. Both have to happen to create a home where faith can flourish.

Perhaps you would prefer a book about getting your *teen* all orderly and obedient and easy for you to manage. Perhaps that's what you're expecting to find in this one. Yet here I am talking about *your* heart, *your* idolatry, *your* battle. I know, I know. This might not be the quick fix you are looking for, but I've found it is the place where I'm most challenged to fully depend on the Lord for change.

Here's the reality: Our kids need us to be clinging to Jesus, looking to him for grace, setting aside our idols, fighting our sin, and walking daily with God. They need to see that our words match our lives. They need to witness a real faith lived before them, one that accepts responsibility for mistakes and apologizes when necessary. We can't be those parents without fighting the battle before us. And the battle isn't our kids. It's *our idols*.

Of course, teens have real issues that need to be dealt with. They have plenty of sins of their own. Their idols will clash with your idols.

But as parents, here's what you and I have to remind ourselves: *I am the adult*. It's one thing for a teen to be flying off the handle and slamming doors. It's not right or acceptable, but it's pretty normal. However, if I find myself responding in the same manner, well, that misbehavior is fully my responsibility. If I'm struggling to control my emotions at 50, why should I be surprised or frustrated when my teen is struggling to control their emotions at 13?

As I mentioned in the introduction, this is hard work—it's heart work. But there's good news: The one doing the work in you is God himself. Listen to this promise in Ezekiel 36:25-28:

> I will sprinkle clean water on you, and you shall be clean from all your uncleannesses, and *from all your idols I will cleanse you.* And I will give you a new heart, and a new spirit I will put within you. And I will remove the heart of stone from your flesh and give you a heart of flesh. And I will put my Spirit within

you, and cause you to walk in my statutes and be careful to obey my rules (emphasis added).

God—not our efforts—cleanses us from our idols. He gives us new hearts and puts his Spirit within us. He causes us to walk in his ways and obey his rules. Because God is at work in us, we can put on what is good and put off what is bad.

As Paul wrote to the Ephesians, "Be strong in the Lord and in the strength of his might" (Ephesians 6:10). He knew that our battle was not against flesh and blood, but "against the spiritual forces of evil in the heavenly places" (verse 12). There is no possibility of victory in our own strength. However, because God fights for us, victory is assured. Therefore, we take up his armor so that we are equipped for battle.

In the next three chapters, we'll consider some of the cultural idols that affect our parenting in the West: scholarship and affluence, sports and activities, and social approval and acceptance. These cultural idols spring to the surface in our parenting, shaping our expectations and dreams for our teens. We mistakenly believe we have the power to determine our children's future and the wisdom to know what is best for them.

As we've already discussed, none of these hopes and dreams for our children, in and of themselves, are bad. Most of them can be good. It's how we approach them that makes a difference. In each chapter, we'll follow the same pattern that we've used in the previous chapters:

- Principles for Parents: Thinking Biblically
- Purposeful Parenting: Engaging Gracefully
- Practical Advice: Living Wisely

We'll consider biblical truth, what it looks like to parent graciously, and how to confront our own idolatry in each of these areas as we seek to live wisely with our teens.

CHAPTER 4

The Secret of True Success: (Isn't) Scholarship and Affluence

Would you rather be smart or rich?

I've heard people answer this question in a variety of ways. But for most of us, I think we'd answer the question with another question: Can I have both, please?

When it comes to our hopes and dreams for our children, scholarship and affluence seem to go hand and hand. We often tell our children that they need to work hard in school so that they can get into a good college, so they can get a good job, so they can provide a good life for their family. While it's wise to be hardworking and right to provide for our families, often we transmit a misguided message to our teens. It's easy for them to believe the equation that intelligence = money and money = happiness; therefore, more intelligence + more money = more happiness.

As parents, we often believe in the power of scholarship and affluence as well. While we may know that God is the provider and giver of all good things, it's tempting to trust in our own abilities and resources rather than trust God. Whatever our source idols (power, control, comfort, or approval), both intelligence and wealth appear to be the pathway to fulfilling our deepest longings, as well as fulfilling the dreams we have for our children.

In this chapter, we'll begin with biblical principles to help us understand how to think about money, scholarship, and overall success for our children. We'll then consider how to engage gracefully with our teens on these topics, helping them to understand the importance of hard work, while not idolizing money or success in school. At the end of this chapter, we'll examine our own source idols and consider practical advice for living wisely before our teens in these important areas.

Principles for Parents: Thinking Biblically

As we shape our thinking about money and intelligence, it's helpful to acknowledge that the Bible considers both to be blessings. The books of Psalms and Proverbs have many positive things to say about wealth and knowledge. As we look through some of these verses, it's helpful to clarify that Psalms and Proverbs are a specific type of writing called wisdom literature. They explain to us the general patterns of life, while not offering specific promises or conclusions for every situation.

For instance, these books explain that wealth is often a way the Lord blesses his people (but not the only way or even the best way). These principles are not meant to imply that poverty or a lack of resources are necessarily because someone is not obeying the Lord. There are plenty of people who acquired wealth through unjust means (and the Bible has a lot to say about them—see Proverbs 22:16; 28:8, 22; Ecclesiastes 5:10), as well as righteous people who lost all their wealth through no fault of their own (think about Joseph in Genesis 37 and Job in Job 1).

The wisdom books speak to general patterns or principles that are not meant to be taken as fixed conclusions or absolute promises. Therefore, we can understand the wisdom of "in the house of the righteous there is much treasure, but trouble befalls the income of the wicked" (Proverbs

15:6) without making assumptions about those who are poor (or rich). Jesus lived in poverty—for our sakes—without a home to call his own (2 Corinthians 8:9; Luke 9:58). However, he was the only truly righteous man who ever lived. Understanding the type of biblical literature we're reading (and the Bible contains multiple types) helps us to interpret its meaning correctly and within the full context of other scriptures.

The Blessings of Wealth, Wisdom, and Work

The Bible gives many warnings about riches, while at the same time acknowledging its blessings and benefits. According to Psalms, wealth and riches are a blessing for a man who fears the Lord and obeys his commands (Psalm 112:1-3). Wealth is considered a reward for the diligent (Proverbs 12:27) and a crown of blessing for the wise (Proverbs 14:24). Proverbs encourages parents to provide for their children and grandchildren: "A good man leaves an inheritance to his children's children" (Proverbs 13:22). Wealth is considered a blessing from God.

In addition to the blessings of riches, the Bible also speaks to the blessings of knowledge and understanding. The Lord himself is the source of wisdom, knowledge, and understanding (Proverbs 2:6). Knowledge is declared to be pleasant to our souls (verse 10). Solomon, the wisest king of Israel, also told his son, "Take my instruction instead of silver, and knowledge rather than choice gold" (Proverbs 8:10). (That might be the answer to our question at the beginning of this chapter!)

In fact, the book of Proverbs was written that we might gain wisdom, instruction, understanding, knowledge, guidance, and discretion (Proverbs 1). These are good things because they flow from the God who created all things. He is the source of all true wisdom: "The fear of the Lord is the beginning of wisdom, and the knowledge of the Holy One is insight" (Proverbs 9:10).

The Bible also speaks to the importance of hard work and the negative effects of laziness. We're reminded, "The soul of the sluggard craves and gets nothing, while the soul of the diligent is richly supplied" (Proverbs 13:4), and that "whoever is slothful will not roast his game, but the diligent man will get precious wealth" (Proverbs 12:27). In the New Testament, Mary and Persis were praised by Paul in his letter to the Romans because they had "worked hard" in the Lord (Romans 16:6, 12). Paul also commanded the Colossians, "Whatever you do, work heartily, as for the Lord and not for men, knowing that from the Lord you will receive the inheritance as your reward. You are serving the Lord Christ" (Colossians 3:23-24).

From all of these verses we can conclude that riches are a blessing, gaining knowledge and understanding is the pathway to wisdom, and hard work honors and glorifies the Lord. Therefore, it is good to encourage our children to work hard in their studies and to be wise with their money. These are not bad things; they are blessings.

However, each of these good things can become a bad thing when they become ultimate things. The Bible also offers many warnings, especially about the desire for money. We want to soberly consider these warnings because for many, the idolatry of money is a persistent battle that births a life of materialism and discontent.

Warnings About Wealth, Worldly Wisdom, and Work

Wealth can be a blessing, but if we start to trust in it, rely on it, and put our hope in it, then it has become an idol in our lives. Our reliance on God as our Provider gets replaced with a wrong understanding of money as our provider. The more we trust in money, the more we love money. As Paul warned Timothy, "The love of money is a root of all kinds of evils. It is through this craving that some have wandered away from the faith and pierced themselves with many pangs" (1 Timothy 6:10).

Paul considered Timothy his son in the faith. He wanted to protect him, so he warned him against the love of money, which could be potentially damaging for his soul. Just like we warn young children to look both ways before they cross the street, we need to warn our teens that money can be a temptation in their lives. Money is particularly appealing because it seems to offer so much: security, power, control, and approval.

It's not that teens should avoid making money or accumulating wealth, but we want to remind them, "If riches increase, set not your heart on them" (Psalm 62:10). It's the craving for money that is dangerous—it can lead them away from the faith and into a variety of trials. Ultimately, the things money can buy will never truly satisfy. A misguided pursuit of money costs too much.

> **Our contentment doesn't come from the money we have, but from the fact that the Lord promises to always be with us.**

In contrast, the book of Hebrews points us to a different source for satisfaction: "Keep your life free from love of money, and be content with what you have, for he has said, 'I will never leave you nor forsake you'" (Hebrews 13:5). Our contentment doesn't come from the money we have, but from the fact that the Lord promises to always be with us. Money can be taken. Wealth can disappear. Riches can't buy happiness. However, the Lord—the Giver of all that is good, the wellspring of life, the God of all creation—he promises to be with us! Our contentment isn't sourced by what we have, but *who* we have. God promises to be our God. He will never leave nor forsake us. He will provide all we need and protect us from harm (Psalm 121).

We want our words and our actions to teach our teens, "A good name is to be chosen rather than great riches, and favor is better than silver or gold" (Proverbs 22:1). We want them to hear from our lips the truth of Proverbs 28:6: "Better is a poor man who walks in his integrity than a rich man who is crooked in his ways." When we teach our teens about money, it's important that they understand we value their character over wealth. Riches are uncertain and fluctuate through various seasons. Integrity provides a secure foundation and takes a lifetime to build. We can pray the protection of Proverbs 30:8 over their lives (and ours as well): "Remove far from me falsehood and lying; give me neither poverty nor riches; feed me with the food that is needful for me."

As we think about our teens and success, we always want to keep our main goal the main focus. My ultimate hope for my children is not that they would be wealthy or prosperous as the world defines success. My ultimate goal is that their souls will prosper. King Solomon (who had more wealth than we can imagine) wisely warned, "Riches do not profit in the day of wrath, but righteousness delivers from death" (Proverbs 11:4). We need bigger hopes for our children than temporary wealth and worldly success. We want them to delight in Jesus, to trust in his righteousness—this is true prosperity and an eternal inheritance.

In addition to warnings about wealth, the Bible cautions against worldly wisdom. It's good for our teens to work hard in school, to grow in knowledge, to learn about the world God has created. However, we want them to understand that true wisdom is from the Lord (Proverbs 2:6).

People may know and understand a variety of ideas, facts, languages, and information, yet still live in foolish ways. Proverbs warns about the danger of being wise in our own eyes (Proverbs 26:12). Pride and arrogance can fester when academics is valued over character. Worldly knowledge puffs up, but love builds up (1 Corinthians 8:1).

Many people study hard and attain knowledge and understanding, but falter when it comes to living according to wisdom. Even Solomon, the wisest king in all of Israel's history, failed to live in light of the wisdom he attained. His disobedience to God displayed his foolishness. We can have all the knowledge and understanding the world has to offer, but if we don't live according to God's wisdom and ways, we're living a life of folly.

At some level, most teens are wise in their own eyes. They may not welcome our advice or they may question the truth of God's Word. But even when we think they're not paying attention, they are still observing our lives and watching how we live. They will know if we are more concerned about their grades in school than their Bible reading. They will know if we desire academic achievement over character. You may think they are not listening to a word you are saying, but they are. As parents, we need to ask ourselves, *What message are they hearing from me most? What do they think I value most?*

It's also helpful to consider the messages they are absorbing from us about the value of hard work. We all want to raise diligent, helpful, hardworking teens. The Bible warns against slothfulness and extols the value of diligence. Yet the Bible also places clear boundaries on our work. When God created the earth, he did so in six days and rested on the Sabbath. The religious calendar of Israel had multiple days in addition to Sabbaths that were reserved as days for no work to be done. Feasts and celebrations and religious ceremonies were part of the healthy rhythm of life.

While we want to encourage our teens to work hard, we also want to instill patterns of rest in their lives. The practice of Sabbath rest helps our teens understand their limitations and reminds them to trust the Lord even with their work. Culturally, Americans live busy, packed lives. We fill our lives to the brink, leaving little time for rest and reflection.

This can create homes with stressed-out teens and on-the-edge parents. It's good for each of us to consider:

- Is the tension in our home the result of trying to do too much?
- Is the pressure on our kids from the culture, or is it from the expectations we're placing on them as parents?
- What hopes and dreams are we regularly communicating to our teens?
- What's the emphasis in our homes?
- Are our words and examples demonstrating biblical truth or worldly wisdom?

God's Word is faithful to guide us as we consider these questions about wealth, wisdom, and work. It also warns us to keep these good things in their proper place in our hearts. As we seek to value God's wisdom and heed his warnings, we will see change occur in the ways we engage with our teens.

Purposeful Parenting: Engaging Gracefully

Years ago, I read a book by a well-known author promoting a "dream big" lifestyle. The book was sold in the Christian living category. She encouraged her readers to create a dream wall with everything they hoped to get out of life. By visualizing what they wanted, they could make it happen. Her wall included a second home in Hawaii, being on the cover of *Forbes*, and becoming friends with famous celebrities.

I remember closing the book and feeling a mixture of sadness and concern. I've lived long enough to understand this reality: Worldly attainment and success do not satisfy. The condition of my heart can be a bigger problem than my circumstances. I know that if I had a home in Hawaii and was on the cover of *Forbes*, I could still be pretty miserable. I'd probably be frustrated about managing the upkeep of the Hawaiian dream home or be bothered by the picture of me that was chosen for the cover of *Forbes*. I've come to realize that I can have many amazing things and experiences, but if I don't have godly contentment, I'm not going to be satisfied.

My sadness about the book was not that the author was telling women to dream too big. My concern was that she was encouraging women to dream too *little*. If I were to create a dream wall for myself, here's what I would put on it: love, joy, peace, patience, kindness, goodness, faithfulness, gentleness, and self-control (Galatians 5:22-23). I want to be a person who exhibits these characteristics whether I'm washing the dishes for the hundredth night in a row or wandering the streets of Italy on an amazing, once-in-a-lifetime vacation. These are fruit I can't buy, earn, or manufacture on my own. The only way I can bear the fruit of the Spirit is by abiding in Jesus, because apart from him, I'm a dry and withered branch (John 15:5).

I want something more than this world can offer. I have bigger dreams. And I want more for my kids than money, fame, and success. I want them to know Jesus, to love him, and to spend their lives knowing him more. Christianity isn't about limiting our pursuits to lesser hopes, it's about pursuing true riches. Jesus came that we might have life and have it abundantly—he wants to give us *more*, not less, out of life.

Christianity isn't about limiting our pursuits to lesser hopes, it's about pursuing true riches.

But misguided messages like the ones from this author's book are shouting at us and our kids, telling us the abundant life is ours for the taking—we just have to work harder, be better, and dream bigger to attain what we want out of life. These messages sound empowering. However, words meant to inspire end up exhausting us. They leave us chasing every rabbit trail of success, only to find feelings of failure greeting us at the end of the road. And, too often, our kids get mixed up in our pursuits. Their successes become our successes, and their failures become our failures.

Sometimes, we create dream walls for our kids without even realizing what we are doing. We want them to be good students, star athletes, and have a wonderful group of friends. Our hopes for our kids can put an undercurrent of pressure on them to succeed in a variety of ways. We may claim it is for their happiness and fulfillment, but often our dreams for our kids are wrapped up in our own desires as parents.

When it comes to scholarship and affluence, we've created a culture that exalts grades over education. As a teacher, I used to tell parents and students that a test grade simply reflects a student's knowledge on one particular subject at one particular moment in time. Grades communicate something, but they don't tell us everything. Kids learn at different rates. Sometimes, it takes a test to help them realize they don't know something as well as they thought they did. That doesn't mean they can't learn it; it just means they didn't know it at that particular time.

We want our kids to develop a strong work ethic, healthy study skills, and to grow in the knowledge of the world around them. Those are good goals. However, our obsession with GPAs and SAT scores can become one of those misguided rabbit trails of success that leave our teens hating school. If we want to create teens who love learning, we need to stop focusing on grades and support our teen's education.

In her book *The Price of Privilege: How Parental Pressure and Material Advantage Are Creating a Generation of Disconnected and Unhappy Kids*, author Madeline Levine (PhD) explains,

> The creativity and flexibility required to become a true learner is inhibited by excessive focus on every inch of progress, or lack thereof. It may keep a kid's nose to the grindstone because she is anxious about her performance, but it certainly does not encourage a real love of learning.[1]

She also notes, "Parents pressure their children to be outstanding, while neglecting the very process by which outstanding children are formed."[2]

As we engage with our kids about their schoolwork, it's important to avoid creating a pressure cooker environment in the home. We want to be available to help our children succeed without communicating that their grades are what make them successful. Our kids spend a lot of time each day in the classroom. Some teens love learning and enjoy spending their time each day in school (I've raised one of those). Other kids don't like school at all, so every moment of their day is hard (I've raised one of those). If we want to engage gracefully with our teens, it's good to have some thoughtful "school rules of engagement."

Don't Be Overinvolved

The level of our involvement in our children's education happens in stages. In elementary school, they need plenty of help with reading, getting organized, and making sure they have everything they need for school on a daily basis. As they enter middle school, it's important to begin limiting your involvement. More than any other time in their school experience, this is the time to let them fail so they can succeed later. That might mean they get some zeros on their homework or forget to study for a test. That's okay! Middle school is the time to let them start understanding that their assignments are for them to do, not for you to make sure they do. Let them begin to take responsibility for themselves. By middle school, they should be able to pack their own lunch, complete their homework more on their own, and follow up with a teacher if they are having a difficult time understanding a concept. Encourage them toward independence in gradual stages.

We want our children to know we're available to help them, but we're not going to do the work for them. Don't write papers for your teen. Don't look up their grades online on a weekly basis (remember, report cards used to be available only once a quarter when we were growing up). Don't pay them for good grades. Don't do for your teens what they can do for themselves. Your goal is an education, not straight *A*'s.

We want to create lifelong learners who enjoy knowing about and understanding the world God created. Too often, grades get in the way of education. Let your home be a place where character is primary, hard work is celebrated, and stress about grades is kept to a minimum. Grades do not define your child. Getting into top schools does not equate to a successful life. Guard against an overemphasis on grades creating a stressed-out learning environment in your home.

Create Healthy Rhythms

While we should avoid being overinvolved in the details of our teens' education, we do want to create healthy learning environments in the home. Most likely, they are going to need your help establishing good routines.

In her book *The Teenage Brain*, neuroscientist Frances Jensen explains, "It's important to remember that even though their brains are learning at peak efficiency, much else is inefficient, including attention, self-discipline, task completion, and emotions."[3]

Teenage brains are still forming. Their frontal lobe is the last part of the brain to form completely, and it's the part that regulates their executive functioning ability. While you should avoid taking on tasks that belong to your child, you can help create healthy routines and good study habits. As Jensen explains:

> Remember, although they look as though they can multitask, in truth they're not very good at it. Even just encouraging them to stop and think about what they need to do and when they need to do it will increase blood flow to the areas of the brain involved in multitasking and slowly strengthen them…You can also help your teenagers better manage time and organize tasks by giving them calendars and suggesting they write down their daily schedules. By doing so on a regular basis, they train their own brains.

A friend of mine once told me that parenting moves from caretaker, to cop, to coach, and then to counselor. In early adolescence, you're beginning to move into the coach role, and by their upper high school years, you'll increasingly transition into a counselor role. Coaches give their players the tools they need to succeed, but they know the athletes have to do the work of training themselves to excel, to build strong muscles, and to have the stamina to endure.

Talk to your teen. Explain to them the importance of removing distractions while they study. Create a place where they can quietly do their work (but that you can also monitor in case they've started playing games on their computer instead of writing the paper that's due in the morning). Avoid an overly busy family routine that doesn't allow time for homework. Give them ideas for success: After they've worked on a difficult assignment for 30 minutes, let them take a break and watch a show or go for a walk outside. Deep mental work usually requires mental breaks. Don't force them to keep working when they're too tired to think. You can help your teen's brain develop by giving them the tools for success without doing the work for them.

Ask Them Questions

One part of creating healthy routines is asking your teen to think about their study habits. Ask them where and what time of the day they learn best. Have them consider what distracts them while they're doing their homework. Asking questions helps them to think through how they learn best. Different kids develop different systems. In a calm moment (not at midnight when a ten-page paper is due the next morning), ask your teen what environment works best.

Let me prepare you: Every teen is going to have moments of forgetfulness. If your child comes to you at 11:00 p.m. remembering that they have a huge assignment due the next morning, that's not the best time to start lecturing about study habits and how inconvenient it is for you to stay up late with them. At that moment, your teen is probably already stressed out. Sit down with them and work out the next steps, but don't add stress to an already-stressful situation. Have the good study habits conversation when things are calm and your teen isn't already worn out or under pressure. Put yourself in their shoes—how do you feel when you make a mistake? Meet your kids with the graciousness you'd like to receive.

Also, during meals or while in the car, take the time to ask your kids about what they are studying. Part of learning is recounting what you've learned, and for them to tell you about their school lessons helps to aid their retention. Asking about the subjects they're studying rather than the grades they're earning communicates what you value.

Take the time to get to know what subjects interest your teen. Understand what *they* enjoy. This will help you know how to guide their educational pursuits. If they don't like academic classes, help them find other avenues of learning that they may enjoy more. Not every kid is meant to be a doctor, lawyer, or computer programmer. We need plumbers, mechanics, artists, and musicians. Asking questions and allowing your teen to explore a variety of educational experiences can help them find places to succeed in the ways God has uniquely gifted and created them.

Let Them Fail

I know this is hard advice to hear, but it needs to be said: *Let your teen fail.* Let them make mistakes. And, let them experience the consequences. The bad grade they receive on the paper they waited too long to write is a better outcome than you writing it for them. Teens are learning important life lessons, and it's helpful for them to understand that making mistakes and dealing with consequences is a part of life. Levine explains,

> Difficult as it can be for parents, it is imperative that we allow our children to go out in the world, to try their hand, to bang up against difficulties, to learn how to fall down and then get up again...By allowing them to get occasionally bruised in childhood we are helping to make certain that they don't get broken in adolescence. And by allowing them their failures in adolescence, we are helping to lay the groundwork for success in adulthood.[4]

I'm not saying be uninvolved or laissez-faire in your parenting. Be helpful and be encouraging. But at some point, our kids need to begin taking responsibility for their choices. We can't insulate our children from the realities of life, but we can be available, helping them to learn resilience by encouraging them to get up after they've fallen down.

We can't insulate our children from the realities of life, but we can be available, helping them to learn resilience by encouraging them to get up after they've fallen down.

Remember Your Goal

When we think about educating our children, it's important to remember our ultimate goal: We want our children to know and love Jesus. That's what we want for them out of life. It's not an elite college degree or a high-paying job. We want to let all that they are learning point them to the God who created all things.

Therefore, don't damage your relationship with your teen by constantly fighting about schoolwork. Your perpetual stress about their academic performance will only lead to negative results. They'll either feel constantly anxious and stressed out in an attempt to please you with their grades, or they'll shut down emotionally and stop caring about their schoolwork altogether. Neither outcome is beneficial for learning.

If we want to be parents who keep the main thing (Jesus) the main thing, it's going to be a battle—in our own hearts. We'll close out this chapter considering the ways our idols affect our views of academic achievement, as well as considering various school options for educating our children.

Practical Advice: Living Wisely
What Really Counts

Whatever source idols you struggle with (power, control, comfort, approval), they most likely will bubble to the surface when it comes to your child's education. They will affect the way you interact with your teen, as well as the way you interact with others about school choices.

Many people view academic success as the conduit to a successful life. Increased levels of education are often correlated with increased material wealth. As I noted at the beginning of the chapter, it's easy to fall into the misguided belief pattern that academic success yields material success and material success yields happiness.

As parents, it's important for us to evaluate the ways a love of money (or a trust in money) is the underlying root cause of the pressure we are putting on our teen academically. Even though we may read the biblical warnings against a love of money, it's tempting to put our hope there. And, if we put our trust in money, our children are likely to do the same. It's ironic that our currency reminds us "In God we trust" because so many live by the creed "In money we trust."

It's not just the Bible that teaches that money can't satisfy. Even modern studies show that materialism doesn't yield contentment. In fact, it's the opposite. Soniya Luthar (PhD) was surprised to find in her research that affluent children had higher rates of depression, anxiety, and substance abuse.[5] Having more money doesn't equal a happy life.

If we are constantly focused on wealth, status, image, and consumption, we'll pass this idolatry on to our teens. Education becomes a pressure-cooker competition to be the best. Your kids are watching you and they understand what you value more than you may think. Rather than pursuing a love of learning, our kids will be competing with every other kid in school for better grades so they can win in the game of life.

Like all idols, wealth and status promise much but fail to provide. A pursuit of materialism actually undercuts education. In addition to higher rates of depression and substance abuse, materialistic kids also have lower grades.[6] It's not good for our teens when we're focused on worldly gains and material wealth. The desire for success can lead to all sorts of problems.

In 2019, some parental dreams for their teens' academic success turned criminal. Thirty-three parents were accused of paying millions of dollars in fraudulent college admission schemes. The federal investigation, called Operation Varsity Blues, uncovered a scheme in which parents paid a college admissions counselor to bribe SAT test administrators and university coaches to get their kids into elite universities. After the plot was uncovered, many of the parents went to jail for their actions. This demonstrates just how deeply parents can be invested in their teens' academic success (or appearance of academic success).

It's tempting for all of us to want our kids to succeed in school—their accomplishments make us feel accomplished. It's difficult to sit through award ceremonies that reward grades and academic achievements when your teen is never called to the platform. In those moments, remind yourself (and your teen) that most of us live pretty ordinary lives, and that faithfulness to God is of greater value. And that's a beautiful reality. We don't have to be the best at everything. We don't have to be the valedictorian to succeed in the kingdom of God. Knowing Jesus brings life to our days—not award ceremonies. Our goal is to hear the words, "Well done, good and faithful servant…Enter into the joy of your master" (Matthew 25:21). God wants us to be faithful with the gifts and talents he's given to us, not to work hard to be like someone else.

In a world that is shouting at our kids that they have to be exceptional in their academic pursuits, it's important that we remind our children daily, "You are exceptional because you are made in the image of God. You are deeply loved not because of what you do, but because of what Jesus did for you. God wants to make you more like Jesus and glorify himself through you." We need to keep this message on repeat, and believe it for ourselves as well.

It's important that we remind our children daily, "You are exceptional because you are made in the image of God."

The antidote to a love of money, fame, and success isn't to forsake all these things. The antidote is to love God more. When God is properly worshipped in our hearts, our propensity toward idolatry will diminish. When we cling tightly to God and trust in him, he will lead and guide our lives. This is life. And this is life abundant.

School Choice

I know we're already near the end of this chapter and we haven't yet discussed school options for your children. Part of the reason for my delay is because I think a lot of our heart issues are independent of the school options we choose for our kids. The other reason is that not everyone has the luxury of multiple educational choices. Yet another reason I've waited is because I've watched kids from every type of educational background walk away from the faith, as well as pursue the Lord with joy. While our educational choices matter, they aren't determinative for our teens' faith. I'll close this chapter with some principles for determining the best school environment for your teen.

What is available?

Most families are considering public school, private school, or homeschooling for their teens (and there are a variety of combination homeschool options, as well as Christian and non-Christian private school options). If both parents work full time outside the home, homeschooling is probably not an option. Single parents may also struggle to make homeschooling viable. Monetary resources will greatly impact the ability to be able to afford a private school. Public schools vary greatly depending upon the city and neighborhood you live in. Some people are able to move to find a better school choice; others don't have that option.

Every family has a different set of circumstances. These are God-ordained and part of his plan for you and for your child. Trust what God has given (or not given) as part of the way he is leading your family. If you have options, as hard as it might be to decide which way to go, it's a blessing to be able to choose how to educate your teen.

What is wise?

As you consider educational options, seek wise counsel from other believers. Ask them why they made the choices they did. Listen to podcasts, read articles, and visit schools. Stay up to date about new laws that might affect your child and your ability to make choices as a parent. Talk with your children and ask them what they prefer. Prayerfully consider each child's preferences and ask the Lord to guide you in all wisdom. He promises, "If any of you lacks wisdom, let him ask God, who gives generously to all without reproach, and it will be given him" (James 1:5).

What is loving?

We also need to consider: What is the most loving option? What schooling choice will help my teen grow in their love for God and their love for their neighbor? We want to be aware that we are part of a community and consider how to love our neighbors well and consider them as we make school decisions.

Ask God to direct you and your family. You want your school decisions to be made in consideration of your circumstances, with godly wisdom and loving hearts. As you consider educational choices, avoid judging others for their decisions. Another person's choice is not an indictment about your choice. Let us be loving as we consider schooling options and loving as others make their choices. Our goal should be to support one another, pointing one another to Jesus, because raising teens is hard enough without us fighting about the best educational decisions.

We've covered a lot in this chapter, which makes sense because academic pursuits take up a lot of our teens' time. In our next chapter, we'll consider sports and activities and all the busyness that can quickly fill up our teens' after-school hours.

A Note of Gospel Hope

Our teens spend a lot of time in the classroom. I know it's easy for us to be fearful of what they're learning and who they're learning it from. We all want positive role models and loving teachers to influence our teens. Whatever type of school your child is in, pray the Lord will give your child older mentors who support and encourage them.

And even though your teen might not admit it, you are still the biggest influence in their life. They might not seem like they are even aware that you exist, but they are listening to what you say and are impacted by your example. The warmth of your welcome, the kindness of your encouragement, and the support you offer will leave a lasting impression on your teen. Whatever type of education they are receiving, your home is their foundation. Each day is a new opportunity to teach them about God, his Word, and his gracious love for the world. It's good news we get to share—and that begins in the home.

MK

Parenting Principles to Ponder

- Money and success are good things, but they become problematic when they become the ultimate things. Money and success cannot produce contentment.

- Concentrate less on grades and focus on creating a healthy learning environment.

- Remember your goal. Don't let a desire for academic success obscure your desire for your teen to grow in the knowledge of the Lord.

CHAPTER 5

Beware of Busyness: Sports and Activities

In *Harry Potter and the Sorcerer's Stone*, a young, first-year Harry stumbles across the Mirror of Erised on one of his nighttime explorations of Hogwarts. As he looks into the mirror, he delights to see both of his parents (whom he'd never had the opportunity to know), standing there beside him. In his excitement, he brings his friend Ron to join him so that he, too, can see Harry's parents. However, when Ron looks in the mirror, he doesn't see Harry's parents; he sees himself proudly holding the school's Quidditch Cup as the captain of a team.

Later in the story, Dumbledore explains that the mirror doesn't show what was or what is or what will be, but it shows the most desperate desire of a person's heart. In fact, Erised is simply the word *desire* spelled backwards.

If you were to go before the Mirror of Erised, what would you see as your most desperate desire for your child? Would it be a life of scholastic achievement and awards? Would it be wealth and worldly acclaim? Or would it be something akin to Ron's desire—seeing your child leading in the play, sitting in the first violin chair, or rallying his team to victory as quarterback of the football team?

As parents, we have all sorts of hopes and desires for our children. As we consider the parenting jungle out there, it's clear that sports and activities are at the top of the list of dreams and desires we have for our teens. We spend countless hours driving from practice to practice, game to game, and recital to recital in an endless flurry of activity. Sometimes, we're so busy getting to the next thing that we can't even remember why we're doing what we're doing. We're just doing it because it's what we do.

 **By doing more, we're missing out on significant moments that happen only when we do less.**

In our rush to and from sports events and other activities, we can easily miss out on important family rituals in an attempt to gain more skills, trophies, and accolades for our kids. By doing more, we're missing out on significant moments that happen only when we do less.

In this chapter, we'll consider the biblical benefits of sports and activities, how to engage with our teens on these matters, as well as practical advice when planning our family's schedule for the year. In today's 24-hour news cycle, with stores always open, it can feel like we are being good stewards of our time by squeezing as much as we can into every day as possible. However, just like our attempts to squeeze into our old high school jeans might result in much pain and frustration, our attempts to put too much into our teen's schedule can result in painful and unforeseen consequences for their overall health.

Principles for Parents: Thinking Biblically

As I begin this chapter, I do so with a bit of apprehension. Most of us will most likely agree that money and wealth can have hidden pitfalls of idolatry that we have to be warned against (and need to warn our teens against). However, when it comes to our national love (or even obsession?) of sports, parents tend to be more sensitive or defensive about the choices they make.

And usually, that can be a sign we're poking at a pretty large cultural idol. So, I'm a little worried about poking that bear and hoping that the "don't shoot the messenger" concept wins the day.

When we think about idols, these three basic questions usually tell us a lot: What do I spend my money on? What do I spend my time on? What do I think/talk about? In 2017, Americans spent $56 billion to attend sporting events. The average cost for a family of four to attend an NFL game was $502.84.[1] The average American male watched 5.8 hours of sports per week, while the average female watched 2.6 hours a week.[2] Sports gambling has increasingly become a national addiction, leading to broken families, lost jobs, and foreclosed homes.[3] There are numerous TV channels devoted to reporting on sports, and some entire channels that focus on just one sport (even golf has its own channel!).

We are a nation who talks about sports, watches sports, plays sports, and spends billions of dollars on sports each year. If you go to a sporting event, it can almost feel like a worship experience: there's communal joy, sorrow, cheering, singing, and a sense of unified belonging. We collectively love the thrill of competition—exulting in the electrified delight of a win and mourning together the shared dismay of defeat.

Like all the cultural idols we'll discuss in these chapters, sports and other activities are not bad in and of themselves, but so often they become the ultimate thing in our lives and our parenting. Let me acknowledge on the front end that there are many good reasons we encourage our children to participate in sports, play musical instruments, or join school clubs. My kids have been involved in each of these. We'll start by considering the good of these endeavors, and then we'll consider some warnings we need to be aware of as parents when it comes to how these activities can affect our families.

The Good News

As Christian parents, we hope to teach our teens the importance of honoring God with their whole lives. This includes properly caring for their bodies, as well as stewarding the gifts God has uniquely given them. It's good to teach teens to eat right, exercise, and enjoy the world God has created. Some teens may enjoy artistic endeavors, others may love to play instruments, and some may find delight in a particular sport. God has created an amazing world, and we're made in his image, so it's right and good that our teens will want to create—whether it's a beautiful painting or an amazing passing sequence.

In the book of Exodus, we read about certain craftsmen who were gifted by God to help build the intricate designs of the temple. Moses explained,

> See, the LORD has called by name Bezalel the son of Uri, son of Hur, of the tribe of Judah; and he has filled him with the Spirit of God, with skill, with intelligence, with knowledge, and with all craftsmanship, to devise artistic designs, to work in gold and silver and bronze, in cutting stones for setting, and in carving wood, for work in every skilled craft. And he has inspired him to teach, both him and Oholiab the son of Ahisamach of the tribe of Dan. He has filled them with skill to do every sort of work done by an engraver or by a designer or by an embroiderer in blue and purple and scarlet yarns and fine twined linen, or by a weaver—by any sort of workman or skilled designer (Exodus 35:30-35).

In a similar way, God has gifted your teen with particular skills. Perhaps they are talented with a paintbrush, an instrument, or a soccer ball. Whatever ways the Lord has uniquely gifted them can be a means by which they can honor and glorify God. While we don't have a temple building any longer like the Israelites did, Paul said that in Christ, our bodies are a temple of the Holy Spirit. Christ lives in us, so what we do with our physical bodies matters: "You are not your own, for you were bought with a price. So glorify God in your body" (1 Corinthians 6:19-20). Glorifying God with our bodies means we avoid using our bodies for sin, but it also means we actively use our bodies to serve others and honor him.

Developing our teens' abilities can help them to care for others. A young athlete is able to help an aging church member with her yard work. A teen musician can encourage others by leading worship at church. An artist can add beauty and warmth to a home. An actress can perform and entertain others with her gifts. An after-school job can develop skills that help serve the community. It's good and right for us to encourage our teens to develop their God-given talents so that they can serve others and glorify God as they do so.

Another benefit of activities for teens is that they gain skills needed for life. As any athlete will know, there's a huge mental benefit that comes from playing sports. It's not just physical. Athletes and musicians learn discipline through their training. Day after day of rigorous training leads to freedom. It's only the student who has practiced for hours on end who can play their musical instrument with delight. (We've all heard the results of not practicing and it's rather painful for everyone involved.) It's the teen who has run sprints and long distances many times during practice who is fit and ready for game day.

As the writer to the Hebrews explained, "For the moment all discipline seems painful rather than pleasant, but later it yields the peaceful fruit of righteousness to those who have been trained by it" (Hebrews 12:11). As our tweens and teens work hard in extracurricular activities, they can learn important spiritual truths. Just as it takes training to participate in sports, it takes training to run our spiritual races. This is why Paul instructed Timothy, "Rather train yourself for godliness; for while bodily training is of some value, godliness is of value in every way, as it holds promise for the present life and also for the life to come" (1 Timothy 4:7-8).

Paul understood that physical training has value. He knew that the training concepts learned in physical pursuits often mirror those learned in the pursuit of godliness. Yet he also was clear on which was more important. While physical training might have great value in the present life, it is powerless to help us in the life to come. Eventually, all our bodies will wear out. In contrast, godliness is beneficial in this life and the life to come.

Sports and activities allow our teens to develop and grow in ways that scholastic pursuits might not. They provide a mental break that's needed after long days in school. They also give opportunities for teens to find mentors and people they can learn from, hopefully about more than just their activity. When sports and activities are kept in check, they can be beneficial for enabling our teens to grow their skills, learn discipline, develop mentors, and use their gifts to serve others.

The Hard Reality

While sports and activities do a lot of good for our children, it's also evident that kids are buckling under the weight of too many activities. It's tough for parents to determine limits, because each child is different, so it's hard to come up with clear guidelines for how much is too much. Some children are able to balance a difficult academic schedule and a sport every season. Some teens need more rest than others. Some teens love to be around people all the time, while others need alone time.

Whatever choices we make as parents, it's important to remember that our teens need our guidance. They may think they can do more than they actually can do. Or, they may be overly timid and need our encouragement to take a risk and try out for a team. You know your child better than anyone. Prayerfully consider your family schedule. Listen to your teens—both their words and their actions. If your teens are frequently in tears or exhausted all the time, they are communicating to you that *it's time to slow down*. Don't let your teens set the pace in your home. You have a better understanding of what is most important, and they need your help to make wise decisions.

We need to focus on raising the children we have, not the children we wish we had.

It's also a reality that you'll have to battle your own expectations as a parent. Perhaps you loved violin as a child and you want your teen to love it as much as you did. But they don't. Or maybe you were the star soccer player in high school, but your teen prefers swimming. We all have to guard against wanting to raise kids in our own image. Just because you enjoyed an activity doesn't mean it's right for your teen. Just because you worked a job and played a sport and made straight *A*'s doesn't mean those are reasonable expectations for your child.

As parents, we are called to love and encourage our teens, not attempt to satisfy our longings through them. We need to focus on raising the children we have, not the children we wish we had. It's a gift to our children when we celebrate their unique abilities and help foster their understanding of the beautiful ways God fashioned and formed them. We have to let go of our own expectations and let God reveal our children's strengths and weaknesses. If we keep trying to fashion them into our own hopes and dreams, our kids will suffer, and we will fail to honor the wonderful ways the Lord made them (Psalm 139:13-16).

Purposeful Parenting: Engaging Gracefully

As we think through family schedules and the ways we hope to interact with our teens on these issues, there are a few principles that can guide us. We want to engage graciously as we lead our teens, while listening carefully to what they are telling us. Here are a few important points to consider.

Listen to Your Teen

As you interact with your child about sports, jobs, activities, and social engagements, it's important to listen to them. Ask them questions: What activity do you enjoy the most? Why? What activity is the least enjoyable for you? Why? You want to get a sense from your teen what they enjoy and why they like to participate. Understanding their preferences and reasons in calm moments will help you to evaluate best practices when life gets stressful.

You also want to listen to what their body is telling them. I know that may sound odd, but if your child is constantly getting sick, losing or gaining large amounts of weight, falling asleep at the dinner table, or struggling to manage their emotions in a healthy way, they are communicating that something is wrong. They may want to do five activities, but their bodies will convey their inability to manage such a schedule. Just like your toddler might get all out of sorts and have a tantrum right before a nap, your teen will demonstrate their exhaustion. It might show up in different ways for different kids, but be on the lookout. If your child isn't healthy—physically, emotionally, or spiritually—it's time to reconsider your family schedule.

Beware of Compare

As parents, we're tempted to look to other families for guidelines to determine what our family should be doing. You may see on Instagram that another teen is running track and working a job and managing a tough school schedule. It's tempting to compare our teen to the other teens around them.

We also have to be careful about comparing them to ourselves. As parents, we have to guard against our expectations of the sports our kids should pursue, the clubs they should join, and the instruments they should play. You may look back on your teenage years and wish your parents had pushed you harder. Maybe you think you could have played a sport in college if they had hired a coach for private lessons. Maybe you believe you could have gotten into the college of your dreams if you had a few more activities on your college resume. Sometimes our regrets can become dreams we dream for our children. We fear letting them down, so we push harder to give them every opportunity possible.

If we want to raise healthy teens, we have to fight against our tendency to compare. Perhaps they'll never be the star athlete that you were back in the day, but you can still celebrate their contribution to the team. You may think your teen doesn't care what you think (and they may act like they don't care), but they can tell what you value. They will know if they disappoint you. Guard your words. Be slow to speak and take the time to listen to them. You don't want to push an activity on your teen because they want to please you. Make sure to communicate as clearly as possible that you want them to participate because they enjoy the activity, not because they want to win your approval.

Value Character over Competitiveness

When it comes to sports, not many trophies are given out for having a good attitude. Or for helping the opposing teammate who fell down. Or for cheering your teammates on while you sit on the bench, game after game.

One of the greatest gifts you can give your teen is to value their character over their performance. I'll never forget a book I read as a child, titled *Tennis Shoes*, by Noel Streatfeild. The main character was an amazing tennis player. During one match, she wasn't playing well, and in a fit of anger, she threw her racquet on the ground. Eventually, she rallied back and won the match. However, when she looked in the stands, her parents were no longer there. When she got home, they didn't congratulate her on the win. Instead, they told her how disappointed they were that she behaved poorly on the court. They valued her character over her performance.

I eventually went on to be a tennis player in high school and I never forgot that lesson. It made me want to play the sport with personal integrity as my highest value, not winning. Of course, there's nothing wrong with celebrating a win or congratulating our teen on playing well. We want to give them all the encouragement we can. However, we want to communicate to our teen that we value *how* they play more than whether they win or lose. Character trumps competitiveness.

One of the greatest gifts you can give your teen is to value their character over their performance.

When your child succeeds, pay attention. Often, we notice how they are doing when they lose a game, but it's just as important to be aware of how they think about themselves when they win. Pride can lead to a lack of kindness, a critical spirit, or impatience with others. It can also lead them to become overly self-focused or consumed by their performance. Pride is always hungry for the next big success, for one more accolade. It's dangerous. In contrast, humility considers the success of others and overflows with kindness, gentleness, patience, and love. We want to foster these attributes in our children.

As your teen participates in various activities, take the time to notice and commend their character. Comment on their hard work, their support for other teammates, their willingness to try something new, and their good attitude. We teach our children as much by what we praise as by what we correct. Look for good character qualities and praise them. Most likely, no one else will give them a trophy for good character, but such behavior honors God and is worthy of your notice and encouragement.

It's Okay to Quit

There's a time to push our kids. We want to raise teens with grit—who have the ability to be steadfast, hardworking, and honor their commitments. However, as we listen to and engage with our teens, that doesn't mean we leave all the decisions up to them. We don't let them quit a sports team because of one tough day or stop playing an instrument because of one week of boredom.

At the same time, we have to be aware of the "sunk-cost fallacy." Sometimes as parents, we are reluctant to let our children quit a sport or instrument or club because they've already invested so much time and energy into it. However, that time is already gone. We shouldn't force our teens to keep playing a musical instrument simply because they've already been playing it for three years. We shouldn't try to manipulate them into continuing by saying things like, "Well, I guess all those years of driving you to practice was a complete waste of my time." Statements like that will weigh heavily on kids and might guilt-trip them into continuing, but could also bring about a lot of resentment.

In contrast, it's helpful to view all the various activities for your kids as opportunities to figure out what they enjoy. Don't expect them to become a specialist at age 11 in any sport, instrument, or activity. It's actually healthier for them to be allowed to experience a range of activities so that they will be able to figure out what they're good at. Don't assume your child doesn't have grit simply because they stop playing an instrument. It's possible they haven't found what they are willing to devote a lot of time and energy to.

In his book *Range,* David Epstein tells the story of American jazz pianist and composer Duke Ellington. When Ellington was seven, he took a few music lessons, but before he learned to read music, he quit to focus on baseball. Later, he focused on drawing and painting. It wasn't until he was 14 that he sat down at a piano again. He never learned to read music, but taught himself how to compose by listening to music and figuring out on his own what he liked.[4] Quitting at seven didn't limit Ellington. It allowed him time to explore other pursuits until he came back to the piano on his own, with an internal motivation to excel.

Sometimes as parents, we mistakenly think it's our job to motivate our kids, especially in areas which they show natural ability or talent. But that's not the key to their success. Our teens need internal motivation (not external pressure from us) if they are going to succeed.

In fact, most elite athletes don't get their start by spending a lot of time specializing in one sport or activity. Epstein notes, "They play a variety of sports, usually in an unstructured or lightly structured environment; they gain a range of physical proficiencies from which they can draw; they learn about their own abilities and proclivities; and only later do they focus in and ramp up technical practice in one area."[5] For an athlete to try new things and develop a range of skills usually means quitting one activity and engaging in another. And (this is really good news!), you don't need to hire a private baseball pitching coach at age seven for your child to succeed.

Ultimately, there's a time for grit, and there's a time to quit. It's going to take discernment, wisdom, and insight into our kids to know which to encourage at what time in their lives. Don't let what they've already invested in an activity force them to continue it just for the sake of it. Talk to your teen, consider your family's schedule, and make the decisions that work best for you all from year to year. Involving your teen in this evaluation process will help them begin to develop strong decision-making skills for the future. We all need to learn when to say no so that we can rightly choose when to say yes. Our kids need to learn the value of saying no as much as they need to learn the value of hard work and commitment.

The Benefits of Boredom

As parents of teens, we can feel a lot like a hamster running on a wheel. We rush and rush and rush, and sometimes we don't feel like we're getting anywhere. All of a sudden, it's tomorrow, and we're rushing and rushing all over again. If I could invite you to add anything to your schedule, it would be a little bit of boredom.

In our modern era that stresses productivity, we've lost our appreciation for the value of teens having time to let their minds wander, explore outside, and be a little bored. Some of this comes from a fear that kids who are left on their own might get into trouble, and that's possible. But some generally supervised boredom can be good for kids.

When my kids were young, every afternoon, they had an hour of room time. Each of them went to their rooms and played on their own. They rarely wanted this time to themselves, but I needed it, and so did they. Now that they're older, they've all told me how much they appreciate the time they had to be "bored" because they learned how to entertain themselves. None of them are bothered by being alone, and in fact, all of them enjoy having time to pursue activities on their own.

In our culture of busyness, some teens never learn to develop a hobby that they enjoy. Having free time allowed each of my kids to have opportunities to be creative. One of my daughters loved to draw beautiful letters and paint, my son built his own bookshelf out of a tree he cut down from our backyard, and my other daughter taught herself how to play the piano and write music on her keyboard. Free time may initially be boring, but it allows teens the opportunity to be creative.

As you consider your days, make room for breaks. Allow time for puzzles, reading for pleasure, cooking together, gardening, and building things. It's amazing what you can say yes to by first being willing to say no to an overly busy schedule.

Practical Advice: Living Wisely

We've just considered some principles for helping us to engage with our teens on matters relating to sports and activities. We'll conclude this chapter by thinking through some questions to ask yourself (and your teens) as you evaluate sports and activities within your family. Before your teens sign up for that team, commit to that club, or take on that after-school job, here are some questions to consider as a family.

Why does my teen want to do this activity?

It's always wise to begin by talking to your teen. There are many good reasons to choose to do an activity, and there are some not-so-good reasons. If your teen is simply trying to build up a college resume or please others, this can be an opportunity to teach them about the importance of making wise choices about how they use their time, rather than becoming overcommitted.

Your teen might be choosing an activity because they feel pressure from you. While it's good that they care about your preferences, you want them to pick activities they enjoy, not ones they feel pressured to do. Encourage your teen to use their after-school hours to pursue what interests them. Let them use that time to help them develop into a whole person—one who works diligently at school and also invests in activities they enjoy. This pattern will set them up well for life.

At the same time, it's okay to encourage your teen toward an activity they may not initially want to do or are fearful to try. One fall, we encouraged one of our daughters to run cross country. It was challenging for her, but she stuck with it. She came away from the season with a new confidence, both physically and mentally. Even though there were many days she didn't want to run, she learned to persevere. At some points, you may encourage your teen to participate in an activity they may not want to do at first, just so they can gain experience and learn whether any interest will develop.

We don't want our teens to be overcommitted and continually exhausted. Nor do we want them to quit an activity at the first sign of boredom or fatigue. You know your teen. One teen might need to hear "It's okay to stop." Another teen might need to hear "You can do this!" Prayerfully consider each child and each situation.

In addition, talk through the pros and cons of any activity with your child. It's important that they are involved in the decision-making process because that's part of the learning experience too. Before they commit, have a conversation. Teaching them to think through time management while in high school will help them to prepare for managing their time as adults.

Will this activity prevent healthy sleep habits?

One of the most important lessons we can teach our teen is that they are limited. They may feel energized and excited when they first sign up for that team or club, but each of us can only do so much. Our bodies are made to need sleep. And research shows that teens need a lot of sleep for healthy development. In fact, it's recommended that the average adolescent get nine-and-a-quarter hours of sleep per night. However, most American teens get less than six-and-a-half hours a night.[6]

In *The Teenage Brain*, Jensen explains, "A lack of good sleep habits results in much more than a tired body and mind. It can have profound and lasting effects on teenagers and could contribute to everything from juvenile delinquency to depression, obesity, high blood pressure, and cardiovascular disease."[7]

Overly busy schedules contribute to the problem. Teens rise early to get to school, they rush to after-school activities, and then they stay up late doing homework. They carry a crushing schedule, with negative outcomes: "Sleep deprivation increases the likelihood teens will suffer myriad negative consequences, including an inability to concentrate, poor grades, drowsy-driving incidents, anxiety, depression, thoughts of suicide and even suicide attempts."[8]

Years ago, you used to observe your two-year old's tantrums and know, *Wow, this child really needs a nap!* Our teens are in chronic need of rest. And it's not because they are lazy. Teenagers have different physical needs than adults. Encourage them to sleep in on Saturdays and take naps when they can. As you choose activities with your teen, make sure there will be enough time for them to get the sleep they need—it's one of the best activities we can give them.

Will this activity keep us out of church regularly?

In our modern era of travel sports, it's common for practices and games to take up a good portion of the week, as well as the weekend. One important point to consider before committing to a travel team is to ask about the impact it will have on your family's weekly church attendance. If you have multiple kids involved in travel sports, that will most likely impact your ability to be at church together as a family on a regular basis.

As you consider what you are preparing your teens for in life, don't neglect the importance of church. It's not that we want to create an impossible standard—we all will miss church at times for valid reasons. However, we want to model for our teens that church is our priority. So you have to ask: Will regular weekend travel be required?

It's important to remember that many of our kids may play sports for a season, and the majority of them won't play beyond high school. The NCAA reports that only 6 percent of high school athletes play in college. Only 2 percent of college athletes go on to professional sports.[9] That means they have about a .12 percent chance of becoming a professional athlete. However, 26 percent of parents hope their child will one day become a professional athlete.[10] Our sports dreams for our kids don't match the likely outcome.

Our misguided hopes can have a negative impact on our ability to make wise decisions when it comes to our teens. It's important that we help our teens choose what is best. As we discussed in chapter 3, our kids benefit from regular church attendance. They need to hear the Word taught each week, as well as fellowship with God's people. These are activities to prioritize in their lives. Doing that will help set a pattern we want them to continue, particularly as they head off to college. As you consider sports and activities, make sure to assess how they will impact your teens' ability to be involved in the life of the church.

Will this activity interfere with family dinners?

Families need regular routines and time together. Shared family meals are particularly important, especially during the teen years. However, it can become increasingly difficult to find time to all eat together when everyone is running in a thousand different directions. As you consider your family's schedule, family meals are an important priority. Levine explains:

> Perhaps the single most important ritual a family can observe is having dinner together. Families who eat together five or more

times a week have kids who are significantly less likely to use tobacco, alcohol, or marijuana, have higher grade-point averages, less depressive symptoms, and fewer suicide attempts than families who eat together two or fewer times a week. [11]

Sharing a meal together allows for opportunities to catch up on one another's day, share stories, and pray together. While such interaction might not seem significant, these small moments leave a big impact—whether they take place during breakfast, lunch, dinner, or dessert. Some of the times we've belly laughed the hardest have been when we're all sitting around the table together. Our kids chat with one another, and we get to hear their conversations. They tend to share more when talking with one another, which allows us to be able to ask follow-up questions at other times during the day. While family meals together aren't spectacular moments our teens will necessarily remember, they help provide our teens with a deep sense of belonging and routine.

Meals together are also a good opportunity for kids to learn to lend a helping hand and work together to clean up after dinner. While it would actually be easier for me to clean up quietly on my own and let the kids go off to finish their homework, it's important for teens to contribute to helping out the family. Chores are life skills that our kids need to learn (and their future roommates and spouses will thank you!).

While family meals together aren't spectacular moments our teens will necessarily remember, they help provide our teens with a deep sense of belonging and routine.

As you consider activities, make sure to think about how they will impact family dinners. While we all have weeks when we're eating fast food on the go, we don't want to make that the regular pattern of our homes. Saying no to too many activities can help us say yes more often to the important ritual of eating meals together as a family.

Will this activity prevent free time?

Our kids need free time to do their homework, have a social life, and serve in their community. Unstructured time allows them to volunteer, go for a hike, and hang out with friends. We want them to have the opportunity to pursue the activities they enjoy, but we also want to allow them to have space in their schedule to be able to serve others.

One way we tried to create availability in our kids' schedules was to keep the winter season free from activities. November, December, and January are often pretty busy, so it was always helpful to have everyone home from school by 3:30 during those winter months. That break allowed for family dinners every night, time to catch up on school projects, the availability to go cheer on other sports teams at school, and opportunities to volunteer. It also allowed us time to rest after a busy fall and prepare for all the spring activities.

Having a family "off" season allowed opportunities to sit by the fire, do puzzles, bake cookies, and enjoy being together. Our teens want our presence more than we realize. Sometimes as parents, we can be physically present with our children, but mentally, we're thinking about the next activity we're taking them to. Having some family free time allows us to be emotionally present with them during these important years.

You may look at the list of questions above and wonder if you should have your teen quit activities altogether. I hope that's not the takeaway. Our family has loved the friendships we've made through sports teams, violin lessons, and school plays. I would prefer to watch my kids and their friends play soccer than go to a professional sporting event any day of the week.

It's exciting to get to cheer them on, watch them score a goal, and see the friendships they are making with their teammates.

Sports, musical instruments, clubs, jobs, and other activities can help our kids learn discipline, build friendships, and grow in their understanding and use of their unique talents and abilities. We want to foster those opportunities, while, at the same time, being aware that for every activity they commit to, there might be unforeseen consequences. Our role as parents isn't to choose or limit all their activities, but to help them make thoughtful and careful decisions. We're preparing them for college days and life away from home, and we want them to be wise as they manage their time.

A Note of Gospel Hope

Some days it seems like we've made a new competitive sport out of the question, Who is the busiest? Raising teens is a pressure-cooker environment. We may feel like other families around us are doing so much, and we're struggling just to keep up. Let me encourage you: *It's okay to be different.* Your family is your family. You get to choose the type of schedule you value.

I know it's not easy. It's hard to make choices that seem out of line with what others around us are doing. But, let me encourage you: You know your kids best. Choose a pace that is healthy for you all. Spend time together. Enjoy meals together. Go to church. These are activities you'll never regret prioritizing.

Trust in the Lord. He will guide you. Take some time today to reflect and pray. What can you say no to so that you can say yes to something better?

May God's wisdom guide you!

MK

Parenting Principles to Ponder

- Each teen has unique gifts and abilities that we can help develop.

- When it comes to schedules and activities, avoid comparing yourself to other families.

- Leave room for generally supervised boredom. It fosters learning and creativity.

CHAPTER 6

The Pitfalls of Popularity: Social Acceptance

I don't remember much about my first day of high school. I can't remember where my locker was located or who taught my homeroom or what I wore (although since it was the 1980s, it was most likely an oversized T-shirt with some stone-washed mom jeans). However, the one thing I can remember (like it was yesterday) is that I was dreading lunchtime. Most of my middle school friends were assigned to a different high school, so I knew only a few people at my new school. Of the friends I knew, none of them had the same lunch period I had.

After I meandered through the lunch line and put together a tray of food, I had the dreaded experience of looking around and wondering to myself: *Where am I going to sit?* Everywhere I turned, it appeared that everyone else knew someone. Groups formed as old friends hugged and chatted, excited to be together. I stood there having no idea where to sit.

As I surveyed the room, I saw an acquaintance from middle school sitting by himself. I walked over and asked if I could join him, to which he thankfully replied, "Of course!" It was a relief to have someone to talk to, and we continued to eat lunch together for those first few weeks of school.

Most of us have had those moments of insecurity when we wonder: *Where do I fit in? Will other people accept me? Who are my friends?* As we watch our kids walk into new environments in middle school and high school, some of our own fears about social acceptance may rise to the surface.

We want our kids to fit in socially and to be accepted. We hope they'll make lasting friendships. Yet as a parent of a teen, it's difficult to know how to encourage healthy relationships with other teens in a world of smartphones and electronic devices. It's tough to know what to do when worldly values contradict Christian values, and our kids are caught in the crossfire. In this chapter, we'll consider biblical principles to guide us as parents, how to engage gracefully with our kids, and practical advice on cell phones, curfews, and dating relationships.

Principles for Parents: Thinking Biblically

As we consider our desires for our children socially, it's helpful to take a moment to examine what we value as parents. We may value a particular type of social standing because of our upbringing. We may hope that our child is the life of the party or the class president or the captain of the football team. We may have some version of "Popular" from the Broadway musical *Wicked* ringing in our ear that impacts what we're prioritizing with our teen. When it comes to social acceptance for your child, it's good to consider: What are you hoping for, and why?

For some of us, our hope is that our children will experience the deep friendships we enjoyed during our high school years. Others of us may desperately want our children to have the friendships or social acceptance we never had. Whichever of the four source idols we are battling—approval, power, comfort, or control—our fears and desires are likely to come to the surface as our children engage socially. We have to battle our own desires, fears, and failures so we can help them navigate a complex social world. As Levine encourages, "Being free enough from your own preoccupations to be attuned to the needs of your particular child is one of the greatest contributions to their healthy psychological development you can make."[1]

As parents, our goal is to anchor ourselves to God's truth in such a way that we can offer our teens a safe haven from the storms of social stress.

Part of helping our teens engage socially is letting go of our own insecurities and listening to their struggles with a calming presence. If teens sense our anxiety about their social acceptance, they will either grow increasing anxious themselves or they may stop talking about their social life altogether because they don't want to feel like they are failing us in some way.

As parents, our goal is to anchor ourselves to God's truth in such a way that we can offer our teens a safe haven from the storms of social stress. We need the biblical lens of truth firmly guiding us as we interact with them when they don't get invited to prom or a sleepover or their used-to-be best friend's party.

If we're going to be parents who raise children who can swim against the cultural tides, we are going to have to swim against them ourselves. The psalmist reminds us, "Blessed are those whose strength is in you, whose hearts are set on pilgrimage" (Psalm 84:5 NIV). Living as "pilgrim" parents will require us to find our strength in God and our trust in his Word. Just as it's not easy for our teens to be different, it's not easy for us to parent differently than our peers. Here are four ways we have the opportunity to parent with our hearts set on pilgrimage.

Different Affections

Our pilgrimage begins with our affections. Fighting idolatry isn't about loving less, it's about loving more. As our love for Christ increases, our idolatry decreases. If we want to create a loving environment in our homes, we start by focusing our love on the Lord and trusting his guidance. Paul prayed this for his beloved Philippians:

> It is my prayer that your love may abound more and more, with knowledge and all discernment, so that you may approve what is excellent, and so be pure and blameless for the day of Christ, filled with the fruit of righteousness that comes through Jesus Christ, to the glory and praise of God (Philippians 1:9-11).

Notice that he wanted their *love* to abound more and more—he knew that what they loved would direct how they lived. He also knew that their affections must be guided by knowledge and discernment. Our hearts and minds work together, overflowing in the ability to approve what is excellent.

Don't you want that more than anything else in your parenting? I desperately want wisdom in parenting my teens. I want to know when to let them get that smartphone or when to stick with a basic flip phone. I want to know when to encourage them to overlook an offense or when to say they ought to confront a wrong. I want to know when to give a kind word of support or when to offer a necessary rebuke. I want to know when to let them go to that party or when I should wisely say no.

When it comes to many parenting decisions, there are no fixed rules for the best times to say yes or no. We're each on our own pilgrimage as we journey with our teens. However, we can consider general principles, and the first one is this: *We must seek Christ*. Let me encourage you: Do everything you can to grow your affection for the Lord. Be in the Word, go to conferences, read good books, be in church, and spend time in prayer. Anchor yourself to Christ. It's the most countercultural thing you can do.

As we love the Lord more, our love for the acclaim of the world will diminish. We will be able to parent our children differently than those around us, and we will be okay with being different. We will be okay with our kids being different as well. Love for God strengthens us and fills us with a deep desire for God's goodness to be proclaimed. That's our goal. That's what we're aiming for in our parenting: God's glory, not our own. We can (and should) pray Philippians 1:9-11 for our children, but we also need to be praying it for ourselves.

Different Citizenship

As Christians, not only do we have different affections, we have a completely different citizenship. When I lived overseas, I felt the impact of my "differentness" every day, especially while teaching high school. My Scottish students were quick to point out that it was a rubbish can, not a trash can; a tap, not a faucet; a loo, not a bathroom; and (to my deep confusion as a math teacher) that the letter *z* was pronounced *zed*, not *zee*. I spoke differently, I dressed differently, and I cooked differently. Even though we shared a similar language, we came from different cultural contexts, and I felt those distinctions on a daily basis.

Living overseas helped me to appreciate, in a new way, what it meant to live in one country as a citizen of another country. People were welcoming and kind, but I didn't belong in the same way. I was always a bit different. I missed family. I missed certain foods. I missed driving on the right side of the road. Every day, I knew I wasn't home.

As a parent, it's good to consider: *How does our family look different from the other families around us? What is our true citizenship?* Paul encouraged the Philippians with these words:

> Brothers, join in imitating me, and keep your eyes on those who walk according to the example you have in us. For many, of whom I have often told you and now tell you even with tears, walk as enemies of the cross of Christ. Their end is destruction, their god is their belly, and they glory in their shame, with minds set on earthly things. *But our citizenship is in heaven*, and

from it we await a Savior, the Lord Jesus Christ, who will transform our lowly body to be like his glorious body, by the power that enables him even to subject all things to himself (Philippians 3:17-21, emphasis added).

Paul didn't simply tell the Philippians how to live, he served as an example for them to follow. He asked them to imitate the radical way he was living—as a citizen of heaven. While others were fixed on earthly desires, he was fixed on heavenly realities.

When your teen looks at your life, do they see you living differently from the world around you? How do they see you using your time, talents, and treasure? What type of friends do they see you prioritizing? How would they evaluate your screen time or your social interactions with others? If our minds are fixed on earthly things, we can rest assured that our kids will do the same.

One of my daughters and I had a conversation recently about how different we both feel from others around us. I could sympathize with her and share examples from my own life when my faith has meant I couldn't go along with what other people are doing. We talked about what it meant to be strangers and aliens, and that "not fitting in" was actually a good sign, not a bad one. It doesn't mean we're trying to offend others, but rather, our Christian beliefs often set us at odds with others around us, even if we hold those beliefs with graciousness and kindness.[2]

Our kids need our guidance, but they also need our *example*. They need to know we're in the trenches with them, living as citizens of heaven in the midst of our earthly sojourn. Seeing us live purposefully will show our teens how to respond when they face challenges or opposition because of their faith. It will also help them understand how to process disappointments and difficult circumstances. I've told my kids to view life here as if they were on a journey. When you're traveling, you don't expect that everything will go according to plan. You know there will be delays. You expect to be worn out and tired. You won't always be comfortable. You may miss friends and opportunities. These are all part of the journey.

Our overinflated expectations of this life can greatly impact our ability to enjoy it. If this life is all we are hoping in, then it makes sense for us to anxiously try to create the perfect life for our kids. However, if we believe a new home is coming, we can trust God with the imperfections because we know we're just passing through. That relieves the pressure, doesn't it? A new home is coming, a new day will dawn—that's what we're teaching our kids. Wait for it. Hope in it. Walk in a manner worthy of it.

Different Rules

When we lived overseas, I learned to drive on the opposite side of the road. I also learned a thing or two about roundabouts. There are various rules about how to enter a roundabout and which lane is the proper one to be in depending upon which direction you want to go. Let's just say I learned these rules experientially (after being "taught" by the beeps of angry drivers).

Different countries have different rules. As God's people, we should expect to have different rules than the non-Christian parents around us. Here's the thing: Just because "all the other parents are doing it" doesn't mean you have to. And, most likely, all the other parents aren't letting their kids have a smartphone, stay out until 2:00 a.m., or drink alcohol on the weekends. It's okay for you to set the rules in your home.

Peter urged his readers, "Beloved, I urge you as sojourners and exiles to abstain from the passions of the flesh, which wage war against your soul. Keep your conduct among the Gentiles honorable, so that when they speak against you as evildoers, they may see your good deeds and glorify God on the day of visitation" (1 Peter 2:11-12).

Our goal for our kids isn't just to keep them out of trouble with the police (although some days that might seem like the best we can do). We want their conduct to be honorable, full of good deeds. We want them to be a friend who spurs others on in the faith. The rules of our homes shouldn't just seek to prevent misbehavior, they should seek to encourage behaviors that bless others.

We want our teens to be comfortable living according to a different set of rules. The world will tell them to have "safe sex," while we will tell them "flee from sexual immorality" (1 Corinthians 6:18). The world will tell them to "do what makes you feel good," while we will tell them to "turn away from evil and do good" (1 Peter 3:11). The world will say, "Associate with influential people," while we will tell them, "Associate with the lowly" (Romans 12:16).

As we set expectations with our teens, it's important to have open conversations, to read the Bible together, and to help them understand why we're making the decisions we're making. It's not disrespectful for a teen to ask, "Why?"—that's actually a good question to ask.

Teens may be skeptical or distrustful, wondering if the Bible is an ancient book with rules that don't fit in the modern world. If we want our teens to believe the Bible offers timeless wisdom for every generation, they need both our words and our example. Hypocrisy on our part will quickly undermine any rules we attempt to enforce in their lives.

We patiently teach the *why* behind our rules so that our teens can learn how to make good decisions for themselves. We also want to clearly communicate the reasons our rules are different than the rules of others. We've got a different citizenship, so we want them to learn to live by a different set of values.

Different Hopes

One of our biggest struggles as parents can be dealing with the hardships our kids must endure, especially in their relationships. Because we love them, we hate to see them in pain. Our teens may endure breakups, friendship dramas, loneliness, gossip, unkind words, bullying, and the hurt of being left out or feeling forgotten.

However, our hope isn't in their popularity or social acceptance. As our teens navigate friendships, it's good to remind ourselves what's truly important. There are many pitfalls with wanting to be popular. It might cause your teen to dress, talk, or act in negative ways just so they can stay in the cool kid's club. It's important to remember: *Popularity isn't true community.* We know they need friends, but they shouldn't have to change their beliefs or convictions so they can belong.

As we parent, it's important to pay close attention. If your child is in the popular group, are they aware of other teens' feelings? Do they seek to include others? Are they kind and loving to those who may not fit in as well? Are they choosing healthy friendships that encourage their faith?

If your teen is feeling left out, how do they respond? Do they seek out other kids to get to know, or are they fixated on being accepted by one particular group? Do they attempt to change how they dress, act, or speak so that they can fit in?

How we react to our teens' social dilemmas is an important lesson for our children. It's tempting to want to solve our kids' social problems. If they are left out of a party, we may want to call the host parents to complain or plan a bigger and better party that excludes the other teen. Neither option is helpful. We don't want to add to the drama. Teenagers shouldn't have to manage our anxiety about them being left out.

Sometimes the best way we can help is to sit beside them on a lonely Friday evening. Even though teens may act like they don't want us around, usually they do. However, they may not want a lecture from us on how to be a good friend or a lot of questions about why they didn't get invited. Teens don't want to feel like a problem to be solved. But they might like to go to dinner, watch a movie, or do a puzzle. They may not want to talk about how they feel, or they may want to tell us about every single emotion they are experiencing at every moment. Our teens need us to be emotionally available for them while we set aside our own concerns, emotions, and fears.

As we help our kids navigate social ups and downs, it's good to remember that for those who are in Christ, all things are working together for good, with the ultimate purpose being for us "to be conformed to the image of his Son" (Romans 8:28-29). God isn't working to make your teen just like all the other teens out there. He has something so much better in mind. As those who love God, whatever trials we endure are being used to fashion us into the image of Jesus. Nothing is wasted.

Perhaps your teen's loneliness today will give them a deeper compassion for others in the future. Perhaps the unkind words they heard will help them speak with greater wisdom. Perhaps the rejection they feel will lead them to reach out in kindness to others. We can't solve all their difficult social circumstances. But we can be hopeful, trusting that suffering is purposeful in God's economy. So much so that James wrote,

> Count it all joy, my brothers, when you meet trials of various kinds, for you know that the testing of your faith produces steadfastness. And let steadfastness have its full effect, that you may be perfect and complete, lacking in nothing (James 1:2-4).

When our kids suffer, we suffer. Somehow, God uses suffering to make us—and them—complete. He fills the emptiness with greater fullness so that we are lacking in nothing. He is at work in all things—this is why we can parent with hope.

Purposeful Parenting: Engaging Gracefully

As we interact with our kids on social issues, we will need tenderness, compassion, and kindness. It's a confusing world for them to navigate, and how we choose to engage with them is important. Yes, we can do lots of research and gain wisdom from the advice of others, but during the teen years, it is essential that we ask thoughtful questions, listen carefully to their answers, and offer them wisdom. We're going to need the Bible to instruct us, prayer to strengthen us, and the Spirit to guide us.

Ask Thoughtfully

Kids today are growing up differently than we did. While that is true to some degree for every generation, the changes that have taken place over the past 15 years are significant. Author Jean Twenge did an extensive amount of statistical research on the generation born between 1995–2012 (which she calls iGen). She writes, "Compared to their predecessors, iGen teens are less likely to go out without their parents, date, have sex, drive, work, or drink alcohol."[3]

You may read that list and think to yourself, *Wow—that's great news!* However, the reasons why teens are less likely to date, drive, work, or drink have little to do with an increase in biblical values. It has everything to do with smartphones. Twenge explains, "If teens are working less, spending less time on homework, going out less, and drinking less, what are they doing? For a generation called iGen, the answer is obvious: look no further than the smartphones in their hands."[4]

As we engage with our teens about their social lives, it's helpful for us to realize that their high school experience will most likely be very different than ours. Increasingly, social activity is happening through smartphones and social media rather than in-person gatherings. That might mean less drinking or sex, but it also means we're dealing with an entirely different set of problems. Twenge explains, "The sudden, sharp rise in depressive symptoms occurred at almost exactly the same time that smart phones became ubiquitous and in-person interaction plummeted."[5]

While social media claims to offer connection and community, the results are actually the opposite. According to recent studies, there's been a sharp increase in loneliness among teens since the early 2010s. The more someone uses their smartphone or social media, the more likely they are to be depressed and lonely.[6]

These statistics help us to be more aware as we engage with our teens. If we want to be able to ask them thoughtful questions, we have to be thinking about the things they're thinking about. And they are thinking about their phones.

 **Instructing teens means inviting them into the *why* of decision-making, not making all the decisions for them.**

Most teens will ask us if they can join social media sites. Yours will probably ask if they can join sites you've never heard of before (whatever social media you are using is probably outdated now). This reality is why it's so important for us to be in the habit of asking our teens questions before we make rules rather than coming up with rules that aren't actually helpful.

When our teens ask if they can do something we are unsure about, the easier route is to just say no. However, that response could frustrate our teens and probably won't help them to develop a sense for how to make wise choices. The Bible warns us to not exasperate our children but "bring them up in the discipline and instruction of the Lord" (Ephesians 6:4). Instructing teens means inviting them into the *why* of decision-making, not making all the decisions for them.

Instead of making blanket rules about smartphones, curfews, friendships, and dating, I encourage you: *Have a conversation.* Ask thoughtful questions. For instance:

- When your seventh grader begs you for a smartphone, don't be quick to say, "We are not doing smartphones in this house until tenth grade." Ask, "Can you tell me why you want a smartphone?" Let them give their reasons.

- When your high schooler wants to stay out late after prom, you might want to say, "Curfew is at midnight sharp" (because you want to be able to go to bed). Ask, "What is everyone doing after prom? Will there be parents around? What time do you think would be reasonable to be home by?" Listen to their hopes.

- When your teen becomes interested in dating for the first time, it's tempting to jump in with the rule, "There's no dating in this house until sixteen years of age. It's silly for people to date any younger than that." While it's okay to have rules about dating, I'd encourage you to start with a conversation. Ask, "What do you like about this boy? How did you get to know this girl? How would dating change your relationship?" Get to know the people they enjoy.

Here's what I'm *not* saying: Don't have any rules and let your teens rule the roost. You can (and should) have rules and expectations of your teens. However, the way you go about communicating those rules to your teens matters. Don't lead with the rule, lead with a conversation. You can hold firmly to your convictions while still demonstrating an active interest in your teens' concerns by asking them thoughtful questions.

Listen Carefully

After you ask thoughtful questions, listen to your teen. Listen like you would to a good friend. Be a student of your teen. The better you understand them, the more you can help guide them. They might have a valid reason for wanting a smartphone, a different curfew, or permission to go to a certain event. By listening to their concerns, sometimes you'll be able to figure out how to deal with the underlying problem in a different way.

For instance, your middle schooler who wants a smartphone might actually want to be on the group text that all their friends are on. It could be that another type of flip phone option would give them the social interaction they desire, without all the access of a smartphone. Working through the situation together can help both of you come to a place of understanding and agreement.

After you've listened to your teen, repeat back to them, "It sounds like you're saying…" There's tremendous value in repeating back to someone what they said to us. It communicates that we really listened and heard their perspective. Even if you ultimately end up saying no, your teen will have had the benefit of working through the decision with you rather than arguing with you about it. They might not be thrilled with your decision, but most of us can deal with hearing no better when we feel like we had an opportunity to share our input.

Take a moment to think about rules you have to follow at work or in other situations. Most of us struggle when we're forced to keep a rule that doesn't make sense, just because it's the rule.

As parents, it's important for us to remember how frustrated we can feel when someone doesn't provide helpful answers. We want explanations, and so do our kids. That's normal. It's also normal for us, as adults, to learn that we can't do everything we want to do. We can help our kids to understand the reasons behind our rules by having back-and-forth conversations. They may not agree, but at least they have been given an opportunity to share their perspective. Many of our teens might not have the tools to carry on these conversations in healthy ways. It's up to us to guide them, listening patiently so we can answer wisely.

Answer Wisely

We start the conversation with our teens by asking good questions and listening carefully. Afterward, we try in every way possible to answer wisely. Sometimes this will be difficult to do, especially if your teen is unwilling to listen. They may not want to hear anything you've got to say. I've found that teens respect facts and data more than they respect our opinions, so it's helpful to do some research. If we want to be able to answer wisely, it's important that we do the work of learning ourselves.

Obviously, if something we are discussing with our teen goes against the Bible's teaching, we tell them no, but that doesn't mean we don't take the time to talk about the reasons. For instance, if they want to get drunk or drink underage, that's a clear no because the Bible warns against drunkenness and tells us to obey the governing authorities. In addition to the biblical admonitions, we can usually find secular research that corresponds with biblical truth.

For instance, alcohol use among teens is more dangerous because their brains are still developing. The rule about waiting to drink until 21 is based on reason, not just a random preference. Neuroscientist Jensen explains, "The fact is, teenagers get addicted to every substance faster than adults, and once addicted have much greater difficulty ridding themselves of the habit—and not just in the teen years but throughout the rest of their lives. It's as if addiction hardwires itself into the brain when adolescents are exposed to substances of abuse."[7] We could also share with them the awful realities of teen drinking and driving, as well as the lifelong consequences of one bad decision. Even when we think our teen isn't listening, most of the time, they are taking in more than we realize.

 **We want our teens to understand that God's rules are good and they are meant for our good. God's Word teaches us how we work best.**

We want to help our teens understand that what the Bible commands is in accordance with natural revelation. The Bible teaches us what is best for us, and often these insights are confirmed by statistics and common-grace insights from non-Christian researchers because God's Word is inherently true. The Bible is our guide and final authority, full stop. However, it doesn't hurt for our conversations to also appeal to statistical data that reinforces the reason behind our decision. We want our teens to understand that God's rules are good and they are meant for our good. God's Word teaches us how we work best.

The reality for us as parents? This type of research takes time. These kinds of discussions take time. It's not easy. However, if we want our kids to learn how to make wise decisions, this is part of our job as parents. We ask questions, we listen carefully, and we answer wisely.

Practical Advice: Living Wisely

As we engage with our teens, we all need practical advice. We are faced with new technologies and new cultural issues. Our teens have access to more information today than at any other time in history. They can quickly do research, but they can also quickly access harmful content like porn. New issues will arise with every generation. You and I may feel overwhelmed by our limitations.

However, the good news is that we have access to the unlimited resources of God. And this is what Peter reminds us: "His divine power has granted to us all things that pertain to life and godliness" (2 Peter 1:3). Jesus told his disciples, "Do not be anxious about how you should defend yourself or what you should say, for the Holy Spirit will teach you in that very hour what you ought to say" (Luke 12:11-12). In a similar way, the Spirit can guide us and give us wisdom in how to talk with our teens about difficult issues.

It's also helpful to talk to people you trust. Ask them questions, read helpful books, and ask for their prayers. As parents of teens, there will always be new issues we face for the first time. They will be difficult to navigate, and every child is different. We need divine help and godly wisdom. When it comes to the issues we face today as parents, here is some practical advice I hope you'll find helpful.

Learn About Smartphones and Social Media

At the time of this writing, my youngest daughter just turned 16. Getting her driver's license wasn't easy. She had to take a week-long class, pass an eye test, pass a written test, and pass a driving test. She also had to log driving hours for a full year in order to be able to drive on her own. Our state put all these safeguards in place because they know that driving is dangerous.

I don't mean to sound overly dramatic, but we have to realize the same is true about smartphones—they are dangerous. The data overwhelmingly points to the collective harm smartphones and social media are having on our society, particularly on teens.

Below are some examples from Jean Twenge's research, on the topics of happiness, loneliness, depression, and suicide.

- **Happiness:** "The results could not be clearer: teens who spend more time on screen activities are more likely to be unhappy, and those who spend more time on nonscreen activities are more likely to be happy. There's not a single exception: all screen activities are linked to less happiness, and all nonscreen activities are linked to more happiness."[8]

- **Loneliness:** While in-person gatherings and nonscreen activities help teens feel less alone, social media and screen activities increase loneliness. Daily use of social media increased teenage loneliness by 11 percent, and the more time spent on social media, the greater the loneliness experienced by teens.[9]

- **Depression:** "Eighth graders who are heavy users of social media increase their risk of depression by 27%."[10] "The sudden, sharp rise in depressive symptoms occurred at almost exactly the same time that smart phones became ubiquitous and in-person interaction plummeted."[11]

- **Suicide:** Teens who spend more than three hours a day on electronic devices are 35 percent more likely to have at least one suicide risk factor. There was a 46 percent increase of teen suicides between 2007 and 2015.[12]

These are sobering statistics. I didn't have this information when my first teen got a smartphone. I didn't know the dangers about social media. Honestly, I did pretty much everything wrong.

In spite of my lack of understanding, the Lord guided our family. One Sunday at church, my oldest daughter heard a sermon on the topic of using your time wisely from a guest preacher. He never mentioned social media or smartphones. However, the Spirit was at work. My daughter got in the car and told me, "I'm deleting Instagram from my phone." I was somewhat surprised, so I asked her why she was getting rid of it. She replied, "It's a waste of time and I want to use my time for better things."

This was a helpful reminder to me that as much as I want to protect my kids and have all the right conversations, I'm going to miss things. Technology and society move at a rate that makes it hard to keep up with all the changes. Thankfully, the Spirit is at work—especially through the preached Word, in the context of the church. We may never know what our kids are being convicted about while they are listening on a Sunday morning. That's why the basic building blocks (the Word, prayer, and the church) that we talked about in the first three chapters are so important.

However, if I had known what I know now, I would have done things differently with regard to the smartphone. Here's some practical advice that I wish I had known ten years ago.

Teach Them About Technology

Just like there's a long process to getting behind the wheel, kids need to learn some facts about smartphones before they are allowed to have one of their own. I'd encourage you to have them read a book or two (one option is *My Tech-Wise Life: Growing Up and Making Choices in a World of Devices* by Amy Crouch and Andy Crouch) and some articles or research about the realities of smartphones. Teach them to educate themselves before they make choices.

Have a conversation with your children about the availability and negative effects of pornography (this is a necessary conversation with our teens). Discuss the dangers of social media on their emotional health. Talk about the benefits of in-person gatherings that are smartphone free. Tell them if you have times when you struggle to put your phone away (they probably already know, but it's helpful for them to hear you admit it).

I've seen an encouraging backlash growing among younger teens about social media and smartphones. They are tired of spending their lives in pursuit of the perfect picture rather than taking pictures that capture their pursuit of life. When you give your child a smartphone, you are giving them access to a lot of information. And a smartphone can consume a lot of their time and mental energy. Just like you want them to drive carefully, you want them to use their smartphone carefully.

Gradually Offer More Freedoms

A lot of tweens want cell phones so they can interact with their friends. It is difficult to be in middle school without a phone. Group texts are how young people communicate. Thankfully, there are a lot of good options for beginner phones that only have talk and text features. That's a great place to begin. Later on, in high school, when teens are older, a smartphone might be more appropriate (especially for directions while they are driving). Think of getting the first phone as a way of testing the waters. As your teen earns your trust, they can gradually gain access to devices with more features.

I will say this: The research isn't favorable on social media and teens, particularly for girls. My other kids haven't had access to social media and they've been fairly happy not to have it. If we were sitting down to have coffee together, my advice would be to not let your kids be on social media during the teen years. Instead, I would encourage in-person gatherings. Knowing a few friends in real life is much better than gaining a large number of followers online. Teach your kids that social media is a highlight reel of someone's life. It's not a healthy way of building community.

Be a Good Example

Our kids are watching us. If we're constantly glued to our phones, our teens will be too. It's also crucial for us to be thoughtful about what we share on social media. If our teens are uncomfortable with us sharing a picture or story about them, we shouldn't post about it online. This is an important time to respect their privacy, both in what we share online, as well as what we share with friends. Be careful about sharing their sin struggles, hard days, or embarrassing moments, particularly in group settings. That doesn't mean you can't talk about your own struggles or concerns, but be considerate of your teen as you share.

Confiscate Phones When Needed

One of the rules I set with my teens when I gave them their phones was this: *I bought the phone. I pay for the phone. I can check the phone at any time.* They knew I might read their texts, check out their pictures, or check their internet search history. Honestly, I rarely confiscated their phones. They gained a lot of trust with me about their habits early on, and one of my kids hardly used his (which was sometimes frustrating when I wanted to reach him). But just knowing that I might look at their phone was a helpful way for them to develop healthy phone habits. It matters that your kids understand from the beginning you have a right to look at what's on their phone.

Encourage a Pursuit of Purity

Phones also allow for new ways to sin sexually. While teenage sexual activity rates have declined, sexual purity hasn't increased. According to the internet monitoring site Covenant Eyes, "9 out of 10 boys and 6 out of 10 girls are exposed to pornography online before the age of 18."[13] There's also sexting, which involves using digital devices to send sexual messages, pictures, or videos. And, then there's regular in-person sexual experimentation that's happening among teens.

If we want to encourage our teens to "flee from sexual immorality" (1 Corinthians 6:18), then we're going to have to have conversations with them. We need to get past our discomfort and have these discussions because if we don't, they are going to quickly turn to Google. I encourage starting early and having conversations regularly. It's not about having "the talk"; it's about having many conversations over the course of their lives. You might not feel comfortable doing this, so I always tell younger parents, "Fake it." Go into these conversations like you are talking about how to ride a bike or make a peanut butter and jelly sandwich. Our kids will pick up on our discomfort, so the more natural you can be as you talk, the better. Present the facts as facts. The younger you begin, the less awkward the conversations will become over time. And the more normal it will be to continue the conversations into the teen years.

We want to teach our teens to pursue a biblical sexual ethic. Pursuing biblical purity involves putting on faith in Christ and putting to death what is earthly, including "sexual immorality, impurity, passion, evil desire, and covetousness, which is idolatry" (Colossians 3:5). Purity is a lifelong pursuit, both in singleness and in marriage. Our kids need encouragement to keep pursuing purity even if they make mistakes.

I know these kinds of conversations aren't always comfortable. However, they are necessary. I encourage you to start them at a young age and keep having them. Your kids may roll their eyes or look rather shocked by what you share, but they need to hear about sexuality from you. They also need to hear that no matter what mistakes they might make, they can come to you and talk about their failures and fears. Creating an open door for these conversations helps teens turn to you rather than the internet.

Engage in Conversations About Social Issues

Our kids are facing so many new social issues. They are being asked to tell others their gender pronouns. Sexual preferences are no longer assumed. By the time this book is published, there will probably be new concerns. I already can't keep up with all the changes, and it's confusing for teens as well.

I've found that one of the best ways to talk about these issues with my kids is to ask them what their friends think. It's usually fairly easy for them to say, "This person thinks this or that person thinks that." I get to hear what they think about David's opinion about transgenderism or Sarah's opinion about politics. Before you can know what to say to your kids about these topics, it's important to hear what they think. One teen might need us to encourage them to boldly embrace God's good design, while another teen may need us to encourage them to be kind toward other teens struggling with their sexuality.

We need to listen to our teens, not just lecture them. They need our time and engagement, as well as our example.

If you want to better understand how your kids are processing the cultural information they are receiving from the world, let them speak. Listen well. Pray a lot. Send them articles and ask them what they think. You already know what you think on these issues. You want to hear what your kids think so that you can wisely and winsomely engage them with biblical truth.

When our kids were little, we had to create space in our days to deal with the inevitable mishaps: spilled milk, dirty diapers, and sibling arguments. Our teens need our availability to discuss social issues, smartphones, and sexuality. We need to listen to our teens, not just lecture them. They need our time and engagement, as well as our example. If we want to engage with them, we have to be present. This means turning off our phone. Looking them in the eye. And having a conversation. We don't want our children to be popular on social media. We want them to be present in their lives. Help them to do so by being present in your own.

A Note of Gospel Hope

Some of the statistics I shared in this chapter are tough to read. This kind of information can almost paralyze us as parents because we're deeply fearful of making a wrong decision. It's tempting to wonder what new danger is around the corner or what is lurking in the next social media app. The reality is that none of us knows. I always take courage from these words in the book of Daniel: "The people who know their God shall stand firm and take action" (Daniel 11:32).

We aren't powerless against new technology or against cultural compromise. God's power at work in us is effective. He can keep us prayerful instead of anxious, Word-centered instead of worldly, faithful instead of fearful. Knowing him helps us discern what is best. Our enemy wants to destroy, but Jesus has come that we may have life to the full. He is the hope we have for our children. He can help them to confidently stand firm and take action to do what is right. We can't always be with them, but God promises, "I will never leave you nor forsake you" (Hebrews 13:5). That's our better confidence and sure hope.

MK

Parenting Principles to Ponder

- We should expect to be different than others because we have a different citizenship.

- Popularity is not community.

- Social media negatively impacts our teens. Nonscreen activities positively benefit our teens.

The Blessings: Cultivating a Home Where Teens Thrive

Acceptance: A Home of Grace

Availability: A Home of Welcome

Affection: A Home of Warmth

Introduction

Sometimes, it's good to stop and take a moment to review. We've covered a lot so far in the first six chapters of this book. In the first three chapters, we considered the basic building blocks of a home of faith: the Word, prayer, and the church. We discussed three different types of parenting that shape our responses to our teens—permissive, authoritative, and authoritarian. In the second section, we considered our source idols (control, power, comfort, and acceptance), as well as the various cultural idols (scholarship, sports, and social acceptance) we are battling as parents.

In this final section, we'll think about how to build a home of blessing for our family. We've laid the foundation, we've cleared away the dirt, and now we want to create homes of warmth and welcome. We want the beauty of God's grace to be on display in our interactions and relationships with one another.

Some days, we feel like we're just surviving as the parents of teens. We dream of having a home that our kids want to come back to, where they laugh and tell stories together around the kitchen table. But in the midst of arguments, anger, and attitudes, we wonder if having a family life like that is even possible.

I know the teenage years can be tough—for both parents and teens. You're learning as you go along, and your kids are learning too. Your sweet, huggable toddler is growing into an adult before your eyes (and may at times seem less huggable). In addition, there are so many unexpected turns and unplanned detours along the journey. You're probably experiencing struggles with your teen that you never thought you'd face. You may feel just as confused as they are, unsure of how to guide them and wondering when to hold on tight and when to let go.

In the midst of all the changes and challenges, this season of parenting has so many opportunities. Even when you don't know what to do specifically, there are so many ways to continue to build a loving home generally. We'll spend the next three chapters considering how to create a home of *acceptance, availability,* and *affection.* Of course, we all want our homes to reflect these values, but too often unexpected difficulties negatively affect our responses. Our insecurities, frustrations, and failures bubble to the surface and we react with anger rather than grace, impatience rather than kindness, and harshness rather than love.

However, these three blessings (acceptance, availability, and affection) are the fruit of the Spirit's work within us. We want our kids to feel deeply loved and valued independent of their performance or success. Even in the midst of their worst mistakes, we want our responses to be seasoned with grace.

How do we grow into this type of parent?

We lovingly pursue our children in the way God pursues us—with gracious acceptance, availability, and affection because of Christ's work on the cross. We can bless them in such a way only when we're first pursuing God. We need him to revive and refresh our hearts on a daily basis. As we understand and delight in the love of the Father, he is able to dramatically change us and enable us to love others, especially our teenagers.

We'll begin by focusing on what we all need so desperately—God's grace. The more we understand his continued graciousness toward us, the more we will lovingly extend graciousness to our teens. In each chapter, we'll follow the same pattern that we've used in the previous chapters:

- Principles for Parents: Thinking Biblically
- Purposeful Parenting: Engaging Gracefully
- Practical Advice: Living Wisely

Let's begin. May God's grace guide us. May his love lead us. And may he build homes that are blessed to be a blessing to others.

CHAPTER 7

Acceptance: A Home of Grace

Some experiences from our teenage years we can remember as if they had happened yesterday. I still remember with stunning clarity the day I learned a powerful lesson about grace.

I was working my first job over the Christmas holiday season at a local department store in the gift-wrapping department. For some reason, I was running late. I rushed around the house getting everything together and jumped in my car. I quickly put the car in reverse and backed out.

Immediately, I felt the impact and heard the crash.

In my hurry, I had completely forgotten to open the garage door. As I got out of my car and assessed the damage, my mom came rushing outside because she had heard the noise. She looked at what had happened and told me, "I know you're late. Go ahead and take my car to work. I'll tell your dad."

I took her keys and went to work, feeling horribly about what I had done. I could tell from the look of things that I had completely destroyed the garage door. It would need a full replacement. And, in the meantime, I had no idea how I would even be able to get my car out of the garage.

By the time I came home that evening, I saw my car sitting in the driveway. Somehow, my dad had gotten the car out so that I'd be able to use it.

When I came into the house, he met my embarrassed apology with a smile and said, with compassion, "Girl, how on earth did that happen?"

Neither he nor my mom ever once lectured me about my mistake. They didn't give me a long list of things I could have done better to avoid crashing into the garage door. They didn't berate me for being in a hurry. They never once complained about how much it cost to replace the door.

Instead, they gave me grace. They looked at me and showed me compassion and understanding. They knew I wasn't typically late, that I didn't mean to destroy the door, and that I was so sorry for what I had done. When I felt so badly about my mistake, they met me with loving acceptance.

Can I tell you something about that incident? It still makes me tear up right now to think about it. I still feel overwhelmed by how much love I felt from both of my parents in the midst of my mistake. My mom showed such wisdom by understanding in the heat of the moment what needed to happen first—she gave me her car and let me get to work. It probably was inconvenient for her in ways I've never even heard about because she never complained about it.

My dad must have spent extra hours figuring out how to get my car out of the garage, and then more hours getting the garage door fixed. And rather than lecture me or scold me, my parents graciously covered my mistake. And now, we still laugh about the time I drove the car through the garage door. Amazingly, it's not a negative memory from my teenage years, but a positive one. My parents' response makes it one of the most defining memories of their love for me.

When our kids fail, it's not just a situation to deal with or a problem to solve. It's an opportunity to teach our children about God's grace in a powerful way.

You may have had parents who would have handled a situation like that in a very different way. There may have been yelling, anger, or harsh words. You may recall those types of memories not with fondness, but with shame. We can't change the way our parents met our failures, but we can thoughtfully consider how we respond to our teens' failures.

We begin by teaching the concept of grace to our teens as we study the Word together. It's a primary Christian doctrine (we are saved by "grace alone") and the Word sets the foundation for their understanding. However, this knowledge comes alive in a profound way as they experience grace in the home. A teen's understanding of God is indelibly shaped by the example of their parents. When our kids fail, it's not just a situation to deal with or a problem to solve. It's an opportunity to teach our children about God's grace in a powerful way.

In the midst of our everyday interactions with our kids, some of the most important lessons are being conveyed through how we respond to their failures and successes. These seemingly insignificant interactions profoundly impact your teen. In this chapter, we'll consider a few principles about how we can be purposeful in our parenting, and some practical advice as we seek to graciously love our teens—on both their best and worst days.

Principles for Parents: Thinking Biblically

As our children enter the teenage years, it's important for us to have some general principles in mind so that we're prepared as parents. We want to create a loving and accepting home, but sometimes we struggle to know the difference between a gracious home and a permissive home. Let's consider five principles to guide us and how they can help shape our interactions with our teens.

Teens Will Make Mistakes

I know this may seem obvious, but sometimes we forget: *Our teens are not perfect.* They are going to make mistakes, they'll disobey, and they'll struggle with sin their whole lives. How do I know this? The Bible tells me so.

When Jesus taught his disciples to pray, he included, "Forgive us our sins, for we ourselves forgive everyone who is indebted to us" (Luke 11:4). Jesus knew his disciples would sin and be sinned against by others. They would regularly need to be forgiven themselves, and regularly need to forgive others. Even the great apostle Paul confessed his own lack of perfection: "Not that I have already obtained this or am already perfect, but I press on to make it my own, because Christ Jesus has made me his own" (Philippians 3:12). If the apostles weren't perfect, we shouldn't expect our teens to be perfect.

It's also important for us as parents to distinguish between sinful choices and unplanned mistakes. Driving my car through the garage door was truly an accident. Perhaps it was the result of my lack of planning (I can't remember why I was running late), but it wasn't a sinful choice, nor an act of teenage rebellion. We should take great care as parents to carefully distinguish between deliberate defiance and honest mistakes.

There's also the reality that our teens will make bad choices. They are going to get things wrong. They may lie, shoplift, cheat on a test, disobey at school, sneak out at night, drink alcohol, or use drugs. With social media, we're faced with many new ways for teens to make sinful choices: gossip, porn, sexting, and bullying can all flourish on smartphones. As a parent, don't be surprised or overly dismayed when your teen makes a bad choice. It's also good to be prepared for the possibility that their wrong choices will impact us in negative ways—they may cost us time, money, or a full night's sleep. Preparing our heart for these interactions is vital. Our expectations greatly impact our reactions.

Accepting that our teens will struggle with sin does not mean we accept or celebrate their sin. Going against God's Word is never good for our teen. We want to guide them in the truth and lead them on the path of life. At the same time, we prepare our hearts so that when they fail, we are ready to respond graciously, with the same mercy and grace we've received in our own lives.

My Response Is My Responsibility

When our kids make bad choices, it's difficult for us. Even though we know to expect our teens to make mistakes, we'll still find ourselves taken by surprise. And that leads us to a second parenting principle: *My response is my responsibility*. How we choose to respond to our teens' behavior is our problem, not theirs. If you find yourself yelling, slamming doors, and using harsh language, that's not your teens' fault. We have to own our behavior as parents. Your teens' actions do not determine your response. You do. *And you are the parent*. That doesn't just mean you're the one in charge. It means you're the example.

One of the most sobering parables Jesus tells is the parable of the unmerciful servant. He shared the story of a man who owed an enormous debt, one that could never be repaid. This servant went to his master and begged his patience so that his family wouldn't have to be sold in order to repay the debt. The master took pity on him and canceled the debt. When that same servant met a fellow servant who owed him a much smaller debt, he seized him and began to choke him, telling him to immediately repay his debt. When that servant begged for mercy, the first servant—who had been forgiven a lifetime of debt—refused and had him thrown into prison.

As much as we may hate to admit it, we can often be like the unmerciful servant when it comes to our teens. When they disobey us, we fail to consider how many more times we have failed to obey God. Grace simply means "unmerited or demerited favor." It's favor we don't deserve (and actually, we've earned God's displeasure). But God lovingly poured out his grace toward us in Christ. When we too easily forget the grace that has been shown to us, we respond to our teens with hostility, annoyance, harshness, or impatience.

Consider for a moment how you would want someone to respond to your failures. Wouldn't you want them to be gentle with you when you confess? Loving toward you in spite of your sin? Gracious toward you even when you don't deserve their compassion?

As parents, it's important to keep our own need of grace at the forefront of our minds. This will soften our responses—not because we will be soft toward sin, but because we understand our own lack of perfection. We owe a much larger debt than ever could be repaid, and Jesus paid it all. We want to respond to our teens in view of God's mercy toward us.

So, if you find yourself regularly yelling at your teen and being impatient with their failures, harsh in your demeanor, or unkind with your words, don't blame those responses on your teen. Instead, go to the Lord. Beg his forgiveness. Ask him to change you. And then repent before your teen. Own your mistakes. Don't excuse your behavior because of your teen's behavior; instead, acknowledge your own need of grace.

Each of us needs forgiveness. But don't let past failures make you feel like a failure as a parent. None of us parents perfectly, and that's why God's grace is such good news. His mercies are new every morning and his power is perfected in our weakness (Lamentations 3:21-24; 2 Corinthians 12:9). Understanding our need for grace helps us take responsibility for our mistakes in a way that sets an example for our children.

As a parent, I've had to apologize to all of my kids. Multiple times. I've gone to them and told them, "My response was inappropriate, and I'm sorry." My husband has done this as well. You know what I've found? It's created an environment where we are all quick to go back to one another and say we're sorry. I've watched all of my kids do this on their own to each other, with no prompting from me or my husband. They own their behavior and take responsibility for their actions—with one another, with their friends, and with us as their parents. They have learned how to apologize and ask for forgiveness.

Rules Are an Outworking of Grace

As we consider the concept of grace, it's easy to confuse a gracious home with a home that lacks any rules or consequences. However, a gracious home readily accepts the need for rules (you can only be gracious to someone when they actually have broken a rule!) and implements them in the home.

This principle was true for the Israelites in the Old Testament. Some people mistakenly believe that the law was given to the Israelites as a way for them to earn God's favor. However, the law was part of God's graciousness to the Israelites. In Deuteronomy 5, just before Moses gives them the Ten Commandments, he reminds them, "Hear, O Israel, the statutes and the rules that I speak in your hearing today, and you shall learn them and be careful to do them. The LORD our God made a covenant with us in Horeb" (Deuteronomy 5:1-2). Notice that the Lord made a covenant with the Israelites *before* they kept the law, not in response to their law-keeping.

God graciously gave the people of Israel the law, even though he knew that they would be unable to keep it perfectly. However, the law was still a grace to them: It showed them how to live, it was a blessing to them, and it served as a tutor to show them their need for a Savior (Galatians 3:24). In the same way, it is a grace to our teens when we give them rules alongside warmth and relational engagement. They need both.

As we guide our teens, there's a world of difference between these two statements: "I love you, therefore I give you rules," and "If you follow my rules, then I will love you." We give our children emotional warmth and love because they are image bearers of God, not because they are perfect. At the same time, because we love them, we know they need guidance and healthy expectations.

Again, we want our rules to be a benefit and blessing to them, not unreasonable or overly restrictive (it's good to remember that even God had only ten commandments). We give our children rules knowing they will not be able to keep them perfectly. However, we hope that will help them to grow in their understanding of their need of a Savior. This knowledge is a grace to them and can help guide them to Jesus. Therefore, have age-appropriate rules in your home. They'll be a source of blessings to your family.

Grace Offers Consequences

You may wonder if a gracious home is a home without consequences. However, God's grace toward us doesn't mean that we are absolved of the natural consequences of our choices. If we steal, we may be put in jail. If we are lazy at work, we may lose our job. If we have an affair, our spouse may leave us. God will forgive us for our sin, but that doesn't mean our actions don't have lasting consequences. He uses discipline as a tool to produce good fruit in those who have been trained up by it (Hebrews 12:11).

In the same way, responding graciously to our teen isn't in opposition to giving them consequences. It's important to offer consequences that align naturally with their transgression. If they get caught speeding, a natural consequence could be a few weeks without driving. If they damage someone else's property, they might have to pay the cost of restoration out of their own money. If they use their phone inappropriately, they may have to delete certain apps or features.

It's not ungracious to give consequences. However, it does mean that we are patient, loving, kind, and self-controlled as we offer correction. Our discipline is rooted in love, not self-righteous anger. God is "merciful and gracious, slow to anger, and abounding in steadfast love and faithfulness" (Exodus 34:6). As parents, we want to reflect these qualities to our teens, even as we offer faithful correction for their behavior. Keeping these principles in mind will help us as we seek to be purposeful in our engagement with our teens.

Purposeful Parenting: Engaging Gracefully

Our teens are going to make mistakes. And our responses in these moments matter. When I asked my daughters some of the most important things their father and I did as parents, many of their replies had to do with rules and consequences. How we interact with our children in response to their mistakes are some of the most important lessons we teach. Here's some advice my daughters gave for parents, which I scribbled down on a napkin one night over pizza (from a 15-year-old and a 21-year-old):

- Don't give unnecessary rules.
- When we're mad, let us have time to cool down before talking.
- Be okay with us not being perfect.
- Listen well. Be present and easy to talk to, not angry.
- Give good advice. But don't lecture.
- Tell us the *why*, not just the *what*.
- Initial reactions to our mistakes are really, really important.

I was surprised by the wisdom of their insights and realized how much our teens are paying attention. They also told me that the homes where they observed teens misbehaving the most were homes in which the parents had the most rules and strictest control, or the homes in which the parents had no rules. Already, they were noticing the differences between authoritarian (domineering), authoritative (shepherd), and permissive (indulgent) homes, even though they wouldn't have known about those categories. They could see the different outcomes within the context of a school setting.

The way we respond to our teens matters. As we seek to engage purposefully, here are five principles that help us respond graciously to our teens.

Personal Consequences Are Different Than Personal Criticism

When our children make mistakes, one of the most important things we can do is to be careful with our words. Proverbs warns us, "The words of the reckless pierce like swords, but the tongue of the wise brings healing"

(Proverbs 12:18 NIV). When we offer personal consequences, we want to avoid personal criticism of our teens. It is very different to tell them "You made a bad decision, and we need to discuss the consequences of your actions" than to speak harsh, critical words and say, "You are bad. You never do anything right. I can't believe you did this to me again."

Correction of a behavior is very different than criticism of a person. We want to acknowledge the truth that "all have sinned and fall short of the glory of God" (Romans 3:23), while at the same time remembering that our children have inherent worth and dignity because they are made in the image of God. In our responses to them, we always want to affirm their worth even as we correct their behavior. It's a very different thing to make a bad decision versus being a bad person. (And by bad, I mean unredeemable, like a banana that's gone all brown without any hope of being salvageable.) As parents, we want our language to reflect our beliefs and hope that while our teen made a wrong decision today, they will choose differently next time.

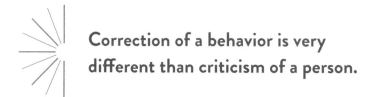

Correction of a behavior is very different than criticism of a person.

Handing Down the Faith explains, "Crucial in the parental transmission of religion to children is having generally *warm, affirming relations* with them. Parents can be very invested and intentional about religious transmission, but if they have emotionally distant and critical relationships with their children, their efforts are likely to fail or backfire."[1]

Teens need warmth and affirmation. Avoid being overly critical with your teen, especially about behaviors that are inconsequential. It's okay for them to go to school with wrinkled shirts, mismatched clothing, and crazy hair—these kinds of issues are not worth the battle. Prioritize what the Bible prioritizes. Let it be your guide and let go of your own personal preferences. It will help your teens understand what is truly important. One day, they will decide to brush their hair and iron their shirts on their own (hopefully).

Understand (and Avoid) Unhealthy Consequences

Consequences are not all equal. Some are not helpful or healthy. There's no need for physical discipline of your tween or teen (unless it is to restrain them from hurting themselves or someone else). It's also unhealthy to use anger, yelling, harsh words, or emotional manipulation as consequences for a teen's wrong behavior. If your teen yells at you, don't yell back. If your teen says, "I hate you," respond every single time with "I will always love you." Teens are immature. They say inappropriate and unwise things.

As parents, we need to have the stability and strength to withstand the emotional storms of the teen years without fighting back. Be firm, have boundaries, but don't get into an unnecessary and unhelpful yelling match. Our responses in these moments are crucial. When our kids are raising the temperature in the room, we want to model maturity by deescalating the situation.

It's also important to avoid piling on emotional baggage for your teen to carry. When they make a bad decision, focus on your teen, not how their decision affects you. Don't say things like, "I can't believe you did this to me," or "I'm so tired of dealing with you." Your teen doesn't need to hear how distressed or upset you are because of their behavior; they need you to be calm in working through the situation with them. An emotional firestorm isn't a healthy or productive consequence. You want to proactively consider your reactions so you're ready with your responses.

When our kids are raising the temperature in the room, we want to model maturity by deescalating the situation.

When my kids make mistakes, I've always found it helpful to ask, "What do you think would be an appropriate consequence?" Often, they have pretty good responses (and sometimes they give themselves much tougher consequences than I would have given them). In addition, it's wise to have a mental parenting toolbox that contains a few consequences that you are comfortable giving. Because once you give a consequence, you need to be firm in holding your teen accountable. Here are some ideas:

- If they break curfew by 30 minutes or more, they have to return home an hour earlier the next time.
- If they fail a test because of lack of effort, no screen time until they've done all their homework each night.
- If they steal or break something that belongs to someone else, they have to repay with their own earnings.
- If they yell or have an angry outburst, they need to go to their room until they calm down.
- If they are caught in a lie, they need to earn back your trust. But until then, you will be fact-checking what they say (by checking their phone, talking to other parents, or asking teachers).

Every teen is different. Some teens will need tougher consequences, while others will feel so badly about their mistakes that they might just need encouragement (especially with schoolwork). The most important advice I can give is simply this: *Choose your words carefully*. Most teens won't remember the football game or party they missed because they were grounded. They may be mad in the moment, but one day they'll be thankful for your faithful discipline. However, harsh words can leave a lasting impression that isn't easily forgotten. As parents, make it your goal to "be quick to hear, slow to speak, slow to anger" (James 1:19). Choose your words wisely—discipline your teens to correct and guide for good, not for harm.

Beware of Compare

One of the most important ways we build homes of acceptance is to let each child be themselves and love them for who they are, not who you want them to be. Of course, I'm not in any way encouraging you to accept them to be themselves in a way that promotes or encourages sinful behaviors. However, beware of comparing your teen to yourself at their age, your friend's teenager, or another one of your children. Such comparing starts in your mind. Take every though captive. Don't play favorites with your kids, but look for each child's strengths, especially when they are different from your own.

In God's Word, we read that favoritism always has a negative and dividing effect on families. In the first book of the Bible, we're told of two parents who chose different favorites: "When the boys grew up, Esau was a skillful hunter, a man of the field, while Jacob was a quiet man, dwelling in tents. Isaac loved Esau because he ate of his game, but Rebekah loved Jacob" (Genesis 25:27-28). Notice that the two boys, Esau and Jacob, had very different personalities. And their parents favored them differently. This preferential treatment had disastrous effects, eventually separating the two sons for many years.

In a similar way, Jacob went on to show favoritism to one of his own sons, Joseph. We're told that Jacob "loved Joseph more than any other of his sons, because he was the son of his old age. And he made him a robe of many colors. But when his brothers saw that their father loved him more than all his brothers, they hated him and could not speak peace-fully to him" (Genesis 37:3-4). Joseph's brothers eventually threw him into a pit and sold him into slavery. He spent much of his life separated from the people he loved most. Jacob's favoritism was a curse to Joseph, not a blessing.

You may find one of your children's personalities easier or more enjoy-able to be around. Another child might be more difficult and harder for you to understand. However, be careful to avoid communicating, in any way, favoritism toward one child over another. It's not good for the child, nor is it good for their siblings. If a child says, "You love Maddy better than me!" make sure your reply communicates firmly, "I love you both with all my heart. I am so thankful you both are my children." In that moment, your teen is asking a significant question about their worth or value to you. Some teens, at certain seasons, may be more difficult to love, but you always want to communicate that your love for them is not based on con-ditions or performance. That's the way God loves each of us, and we want to reflect that in our parenting.

Consider the Root Versus Fruit

Outward behavior starts in the heart. James explains, "Each person is tempted when he is lured and enticed by his own desire. Then desire when it has conceived gives birth to sin, and sin when it is fully grown brings forth death" (James 1:14-15). Jesus said that a person "speaks from the over-flow of the heart" (Luke 6:45 csb). One of the ways we can help our teens start to understand their behavior is to ask questions about what's going on inside their hearts. Not all teens want to talk about their feelings, but some do. It's helpful to kindly ask them, "What's going on?" and not assume the reasons for their behaviors.

One teen may have failed a test because of lack of preparation. How-ever, another teen may have failed because someone said something mean to them at school and they couldn't focus on their work. What's going on in the heart matters. Your teen is most likely struggling in ways you don't know. Ask them questions about what's at the root of their behavior rather than just managing the outward manifestation of it. A desire for approval may be feeding their bad choices. Or secret jealousy might be fueling their gossip. Just like we have source idols and surface idols, our kids do too. As they mature, encouraging their self-awareness will help them understand how to fight sin in their hearts before it overflows into their behaviors.

Remember the Relationship (Your Response Matters)

One of the most significant ways we can build homes of grace is to slow down and say to ourselves, *Remember the relationship*. Don't ruin your relationship with your teen by arguing over spilled milk. Take the long view of parenting. Be careful to use these years to build them up rather than be overly critical when you're annoyed. Don't miss the hurt they are carrying because they are hiding behind a sour attitude. Don't mistakenly believe you can change them by being impatient with their faults.

Open your eyes and take a moment to really see your child. Your teen is a person, independent of you. They are fearfully and wonderfully made. But they are going to make mistakes. Don't lose the relationship with them because you're concerned about how their behavior reflects on you. Walk alongside them. Help them. Be there for them. They may not admit it, but they desperately need you.

The moment I drove through the garage door, I felt seen by my parents. My mom immediately understood, "Now is not the time to talk about this; she needs to get to work," and she sent me on my way. When my dad greeted me that night, he understood that I was embarrassed about what I'd done. I didn't need a lecture. I needed assurance of his love. My parents saw more than a broken garage door. They saw me. They remembered our relationship. And it's a moment of grace I've never forgotten.

Practical Advice: Living Wisely

If we want to offer our teens this type of acceptance in our homes, it begins by accepting God's work in our teens' lives. We need to be rooted in his grace, aware of his providence, and excited about his mission for our teens.

Accept God's Design

Acceptance of our teens starts by acknowledging that they're made in God's image, not our own. Our hope shouldn't be to make our children more like us, but more like God. Your child might love to be in the limelight, while you prefer a quiet night at home alone with a book. They may prefer art instead of science or gardening instead of golf.

Rather than trying to fit your teen into your mold, think of your child as someone you are getting to know. Be excited and curious about who they are becoming. The best thing about parenting is having a front-row seat, getting to observe how the Lord has made our children. Just like we look at babies and are amazed at their tiny feet and hands, keep watching with a sense of amazement as your teen grows. What are their interests, strengths, and weaknesses? How can you help them develop their gifts and grow? Don't miss who your teen is becoming because you keep trying to force them into the mold of who you want them to be.

Practically, this means allowing your teen the freedom to make different choices than you made—socially, academically, and athletically. Listen to their reasons, offer up wisdom, and encourage them. When they feel discouraged about their appearance, or intelligence, or athletic abilities let them know that God made them tall or short, introverted or extroverted, with curly hair or straight hair, outgoing or shy, academic or artsy. Delight in God's design for your teen and invite your teen to do the same.

Accept God's Providence

Not only do we accept God's design for our teens, we accept his providence in their lives. King David understood, "All the days ordained for me were written in your book before one of them came to be" (Psalm 139:16 NIV). When we rest in God's plans for our children's lives, we can stop trying to control the plans ourselves. We can't know what's best for them, but God knows. We may feel lost and unsure, but God knows the beginning from the end.

Practically, this means that we don't try to micromanage our children's circumstances. When they aren't invited to a party, we don't call the host parents and ask why. When they get a bad grade, we don't blame the teacher. When they don't make the team, we don't ask the coach to reconsider.

 **When we rest in God's plans for our children's lives, we can stop trying to control the plans ourselves.**

One of my kids had a disappointing situation where she was cut from a sports team. The tryout process wasn't a good one and the end result was tears and frustration. I told my daughter, "I didn't like how they did that tryout either. However, we can trust that God has a plan even when the situation didn't seem right or fair." I wanted her to know that God was at work even when the answer was a no.

The next year, she tried out for a different sport, and she enjoyed being a part of that team all throughout high school. Now that she's older, she tells me that experience still reminds her to trust God when the answer is no. Helping our teens to trust God with their circumstances begins when we as parents trust God with our teens.

Of course, there are times when we as parents need to get involved, especially in the early middle school years. However, we want to make sure we don't try to solve problems that our teens can manage on their own. It will actually help our kids to accept getting cut from a sports team or not being invited to a party. We can share with them our teen experiences that didn't go our way. We survived, and they will too. We want to walk with them through disappointing circumstances and help them learn from them. Most of all, we want to continually point them to God, reminding our teens that he is in control. Whatever difficulties they face will have a purpose in his providence for their lives. Accepting God's providence allows us to create a hopeful and accepting home for our teen.

Accept God's Mission

A home filled with grace leads us to be a home on mission. We want our kids to understand God's grace is available for them and that his grace came at an extravagant cost. God sent Jesus as a sacrifice so that they might have eternal life. He offers them salvation freely. While it's offered to everyone, it's given only to those who believe. Romans 10:9-10 tells us, "If you confess with your mouth that Jesus is Lord and believe in your heart that God raised him from the dead, you will be saved. For with the heart one believes and is justified, and with the mouth one confesses and is saved."

Jesus is the foundation of grace in our homes. Because he took on our sin, we can be forgiven and forgive one another. Over and over, in every way possible, tell your teens about the mercy and grace available to them at the cross. This is the mission of the church. This is the mission of your home. This is the mission of your parenting.

And, let me prepare you: If you tell your children about this mission and they receive with gladness the grace of Jesus, it will change their lives. They will want to tell others the glorious good news of the gospel. They may make decisions to move across the world to share Jesus with those who have never heard the gospel, or choose a less lucrative career so they can serve others.

How will you respond?

I hope we will be parents who believe with our whole heart that there's no better life than living radically for Jesus. Recently, I heard a college pastor report that the biggest problem with getting young twentysomethings to the mission field isn't their unwillingness to go, *it's their parents' unwillingness to let them go.* It's not a tragedy when our kids decide to give up prosperous careers or comfortable lives because they want to follow Jesus. It's a tragedy when they turn from God's ways and go their own way. We should do everything we can as parents to support our children in godly pursuits.

Our kids can tell what we really value. *Do you really want them to live for Jesus?* It might mean their lives take dramatically different paths than you would choose for them. But let me promise you: There is no better security than walking in obedience to God's call. Our kids will sense what we really want for them. If we are secretly hoping for a life of worldly gains and successes more than a full-hearted following of Jesus, it's going to come out in our parenting. In your deepest of desires, hope for something better.

Encourage your teen with a larger purpose for their life. Pray that they might spend their lives seeking to glorify God in all they do. There's no better life. There's no better mission. That's the fruit grace can bring about in their lives. Pray for it, and rejoice in it.

A Note of Gospel Hope

As a parent, sometimes I can feel the weight of all my failures. Do you ever feel that as well? Perhaps you've been favoring one child over the other. Perhaps you've been resorting to harsh words and unkind attitudes toward your teen because of your frustration and anger. Perhaps you're scared to establish rules or give consequences and your teen is taking advantage of you.

Can I remind you of this? God's grace is enough. It's enough for your teen's mistakes, and it's also enough for your mistakes as a parent. Let the message of the gospel sink into your soul. Jesus loves you. He accepts you. He invites you. Not because you are perfect, but because he has paid the penalty for your sin. When you see your failures as a parent, run to Jesus.

This is our reality as Christian parents. We're not perfect. We accept grace so we can extend it. Don't feel the need to excuse or explain away your mistakes. Confess them. Repent of them. Repeat. We never graduate from our need of grace. We exemplify graciousness by receiving it ourselves. When our teens see us relying upon Jesus, they will learn the source of our soul-satisfying strength: Jesus alone. He's our hope, our strength, our grace.

MK

Parenting Principles to Ponder

- Your response as a parent is your responsibility. Being the parent doesn't just mean you're the one in charge. It means you're the example.

- Teens are going to make mistakes. Don't damage your relationship with them because you're concerned about how their behavior reflects on you.

- Don't miss who your teen is becoming because you keep trying to force them into the mold of who you want them to be. When you rest in God's plan for your children's lives, you can stop trying to control the plan yourself.

CHAPTER 8

Availability: A Home of Welcome

In the early 2000s, Regis Philbin hosted the American version of the trivia game show *Who Wants to Be a Millionaire?* The goal of the game was to correctly answer 15 trivia questions in a row, with every question increasing in difficulty. In the ambitious quest to win a million dollars, each contestant had three lifelines available to help them: 50:50, ask the audience, and phone a friend.

The 50:50 option narrowed the answer to only two choices (rather than four) and the "ask the audience" option allowed the audience members to collectively vote and tell the contestant what answer they would choose. The "phone a friend" lifeline allowed contestants to call a friend—perhaps a roommate, spouse, parent, or professor—and ask their advice. Of the three, I always liked the "phone a friend" option best. It was always interesting to get a small glimpse into the contestant's life apart from the show and it made the game feel like a community effort. However, the ultimate choice for picking an answer was up to the contestant. He or she sat in the driver's seat, having to make the final decision.

As our teens age and mature, increasingly they are in the driver's seat, making decisions for themselves. By the time they are 18, they are legally able to drive, join the army, vote for political candidates, get married, and sign their own liability forms. We can't control all of their choices and may be perplexed by some of their decisions (like wearing shorts to school in 30-degree weather). However, at some point, we have to hand them the keys and let them take the wheel. That doesn't mean we leave them on their own to navigate all of life's complex twists and turns. While they might not need us to help them get dressed in the morning and they may rebuff our words of wisdom, they still need our availability. We want to be that voice of advice that is ready and willing on the other side of the line when they decide to "phone a friend" and ask for help.

You may be nodding in agreement and saying to yourself, "Yes, of course I want to be available to my teen!" However, in our fast-paced, fill-up-every-minute, always-busy society, it's harder than ever to be present. Smartphones aren't just distracting our teens. As adults, we're more preoccupied than ever. Work follows us home, entertainment beckons, and social media distracts—all at the glance of a smartphone.

The availability our teens need from us can't be neatly scheduled into our calendars. We can't plan for a time on Thursday afternoon at 4:00 p.m. and let them know we'll be available to chat. Their willingness to engage happens in random bits of time here and there. We may have to stay up later than we'd like so that we can listen carefully. We may need to get up early so we can help them get out the door in the morning. We may need to put our phones away in the afternoon before they get home so we can thoughtfully consider questions to ask about their day.

As parents, we want to be purposefully engaged, not just physically in the room. (But it also matters that we're physically in the room.) It might seem like the teen years give us the option of putting our parenting on autopilot, but these are crucial years in their development. Our teens need us to help guide them as they begin the process of making wise decisions on their own. This type of maturity takes years of development through conversations that happen as we walk alongside our teens.

A piece of mentoring advice that someone passed on to me years ago goes something like this:

> I do, you watch
> I do, you help
> You do, I help
> You do, I watch

Parenting teens works in a similar way. Our teens become more independent as they get older, but that doesn't mean we can be absent. At every stage of their development, we're involved at some level (doing, helping, watching). As teens grow and mature, our role changes, but our presence remains.

In this chapter, we'll consider the various ways we can bless our teens by being available. Even though teens may act like they don't want us around, they do. More than that, they *need* us around. We'll consider biblical principles to guide us as we engage graciously with our teens and practical advice to help us walk in wisdom.

 **As teens grow and mature, our role changes, but our presence remains.**

Principles for Parents: Thinking Biblically

One of the clearest ways the Lord's love for us is expressed is through the promise of his presence. God doesn't promise any of us an easy, carefree life. In fact, Jesus said, "In the world you will have tribulation. But take heart; I have overcome the world" (John 16:33). We're not assured smooth sailing as we parent teens. However, God does promise that whatever comes our way, he is with us. Before we discuss why teens need our availability, I want us to consider the Lord's promise to be with us no matter what circumstances we may be facing with our teens. Understanding his presence with us helps us to gain a fresh perspective on the importance of being present with our teen.

His Presence in the Battle

When Joshua prepared to enter the Promised Land, God encouraged him with these words: "Be strong and courageous. Do not be frightened, and do not be dismayed, for the Lord your God is with you wherever you go" (Joshua 1:9). This promise was a continuation of God's words to Moses in the wilderness: "My presence will go with you, and I will give you rest" (Exodus 33:14).

In their own estimation, the Israelites had every reason to be fearful. When they sent out spies to appraise the land, they came back with a terrifying report of fortified cities and strong men of great size. In comparison to these giants, the Israelites appeared like grasshoppers. God didn't comfort them by telling them they had nothing to fear. Instead, God encouraged his people with the promise of his presence. Caleb and Joshua reminded the Israelites, "The Lord is with us; do not fear them" (Numbers 14:9).

As we parent our teens, we may feel like we're facing cultural battles and idols that are too difficult to withstand. The "giants" in our land of misguided sexuality, social media, postmodernity, educational progressivism, and increasing secularism walk alongside the "giant" idols in our own hearts—power, control, comfort, and approval. Left to ourselves, we would rightly despair and be anxiously pessimistic at every turn. In our own estimation, there is much to fear as we parent teens.

Yet we are not alone. God is with us. He's an ever-present strength in every battle. We can parent with hope because God is with us.

Whatever parenting problem you are facing today, the Lord knows about it. Others may not understand your struggle. Your life may appear perfectly peaceful to others on the outside, while a battle may be raging inside. You may be facing issues with your teen you didn't even know existed until now. You may feel ashamed and alone. These are the moments you can cling to the promise, "God is our refuge and strength, an ever-present help in trouble" (Psalm 46:1 NIV).

God doesn't necessarily change our situation, but he works mightily through our circumstances to change us.

I know you don't want to be facing these giants. They can be heart-wrenching and terrifying. Your mind may be filled with "What ifs…?" and future fears. However, these struggles with your teens are not problems to be solved in your own strength. They are opportunities for you to put your trust in God alone. These are the times when he proves the greatness of his power. God doesn't necessarily change our situation, but he works mightily through our circumstances to change us.

Whatever you are facing today, God is with you. He is present. He knows and he cares. He is your refuge and strength. God is able to give you all that you need for all that he's called you to do (2 Corinthians 9:8). Don't worry about tomorrow. He will provide what you need for today.

His Presence of Love

God also promises that nothing can separate you from his love. Not only is his power available to you, God's never-failing, always-present, eternal love is with you:

> No, in all these things we are more than conquerors through

him who loved us. For I am sure that neither death nor life, nor angels nor rulers, nor things present nor things to come, nor powers, nor height nor depth, nor anything else in all creation, will be able to separate us from the love of God in Christ Jesus our Lord (Romans 8:37-39).

As we parent our teens, we may face distress and danger, heartache and headaches. We may endure suffering and weakness. But we will never face separation from God's love. He will never leave nor forsake you. He is a sure and steady presence. As parents of teens, we can conquer our fears and failures and walk with hopeful confidence—not because we are good enough, but because God's love is secure enough.

As parents of teens, we can conquer our fears and failures and walk with hopeful confidence—not because we are good enough, but because God's love is secure enough.

His Presence on Mission

Jesus's final words to his disciples commanded them to go out into all the world and spread the good news of the gospel. He sent them out, saying, "Go therefore and make disciples of all nations, baptizing them in the name of the Father and of the Son and of the Holy Spirit, teaching them to observe all that I have commanded you. And behold, I am with you always, to the end of the age" (Matthew 28:19-20).

My greatest hope is that my teens have a strong and steady faith in Jesus. Disciple-making work begins in the home as we daily teach our children to obey God's commands. Thankfully, we are not alone in this mission. Jesus gave the same promise to his disciples that God gave to the Israelites. He promised to be with them. And he is with us as we seek to make disciples in the home. He can provide the wisdom we need for the daily tasks of parenting teens.

In the midst of a world that is pulling you in a thousand different directions, remember your ultimate mission. Don't let fear or forgetfulness get you off track. Live in hope. God is able to make the Word-filled seeds planted in your home help your teens grow into oaks of righteousness—a planting of the Lord for the display of his splendor (Isaiah 61:3).

 **Just like we need daily reminders of God's presence and love, so do our teens need reminders of our presence and love.**

God's presence in our lives serves as an example for our involvement in the lives of our teens. They need us to be present, reminding them that we are with them in their battles, that our love for them is not based on their performance, and that our greatest hope for them is to have faith in Jesus. Just like we need daily reminders of God's presence and love, so do our teens need reminders of our presence and love.

We're made for community. Our teens may not act like they want us around and they may seem to reject our advice, but our availability makes a difference. They are listening. Our presence and encouragement matters. It also matters *how* we're involved. That's what we'll consider next as we seek ways to engage graciously with our teens.

Purposeful Parenting: Engaging Gracefully

As our teens grow older, they can do a lot more for themselves. They are growing in independence and maturity, which is good. We want them to launch into life and be able to take care of themselves. However, as they are growing and developing, they still need our availability in a few important areas.

Available with Physical Presence

As you think about your teen's schedule, it's important to consider how much time they are left on their own. Do they spend hours at home every day without anyone else there? Proverbs warns us, "The rod and reproof give wisdom, but a child left to himself brings shame to his mother" (Proverbs 29:15). Our teens need the accountability of an adult's presence. Even though they may be able to be left alone, we need to be careful about too many hours left on their own. *The Price of Privilege* warns against this type of absentee parenting:

> Kids this age need adult supervision because too much freedom leaves them vulnerable to their own underdeveloped judgment. We know that kids who start experimenting with drugs or alcohol in early adolescence are at heightened risk for substance abuse later. It is important for parents to work at maintaining connection with their young teens in spite of the protest, and even rejection, typical of this age. Eye rolling passes, but the protection that parental involvement confers lasts a lifetime.[1]

This perspective aligns with another biblical word of wisdom: "Whoever isolates himself seeks his own desire; he breaks out against all sound judgment" (Proverbs 18:1). While your teen doesn't need you to be home with them every moment, don't give them the opportunity for too much time alone. Be aware of what they're doing after school and during the weekends. Encourage them to be involved with other people through clubs or sports or work. Too much isolation isn't good for anyone. We all need advice, perspective, and wisdom from other people, face to face.

And don't be put off by your teen's grumbling or complaining about your presence. Your teen's annoyance or lack of desire to chat is probably less about you and more about all the teenage angst they're trying to manage. Don't be easily offended. Be understanding. Be kind. Be compassionate. Your patient and purposeful engagement matters (and they're listening more than you realize).

Available to Teach

Our teens need our availability, *but they don't need us to do everything for them*. Please don't do everything for them! This season is an important time to allow them to learn independence, while still being there to help them. One of the best ways we can do this is by being available to teach our kids how to help out around the home.

In the short term, it may seem easier just to manage the house on your own. Kids generally don't do housework as well as we do. However, if they're never taught how to do chores, they'll never learn. Teens need to know how to vacuum the floor, pack their own lunch, dust a room, clean a bathroom, do their own laundry, put away dishes, make meals, and clean up their own room. I recommend teaching them all these skills before high school. Middle school (or before!) is a great time to teach skills they need to learn.

Teaching your kids to do chores requires your presence. They won't know how to chop an onion or mince garlic without you showing them how to do it. They won't realize just how dirty that kitchen countertop is until you ask them to feel the sticky stuff they didn't notice. They may end up shrinking a few sweaters as they do their own laundry, but it's worth it. As they help around the home, teens grow in independence and confidence. It also prepares them for living on their own or heading off to college (no one wants to live with someone who leaves their dishes in the sink!).

Chores teach our kids that while they are an important and beloved member of the home, they are not the center of the universe. Belonging to a family comes with family responsibilities. While they may complain or grumble, it's worth the effort to patiently teach them and expect them to help out. It's for their good and growth. But it doesn't just happen. It takes time and effort on our part for them to learn how to do things well.

Available to Rejoice and Mourn

As our teens grow, they are dealing with a lot of emotions. They experience so many significant firsts. One day, they may be on an emotional high because they scored the winning goal. Another day, they may feel completely deflated because they got a bad grade. They may enjoy the first flutters of romantic attraction or feel the painful sting of rejection. Some days they may feel like they have all the energy they need to climb the highest mountain, and other days they may feel utterly wiped out and exhausted. They're on a roller-coaster ride, and they need our emotional intelligence and availability.

When teens are experiencing these emotional swings, it's tempting to downplay their low lows and high highs. What many parents consider "offering perspective" can appear to teens as disinterest or condescension.

Don't minimize your teen's emotional responses. You may know they'll survive this breakup or bad grade or sports failure, but *they* don't. In their world, it's a big deal. They are hurting and looking for comfort. Remember that Job's friends were doing pretty well—right up to the moment when they started talking to him. You don't have to fix what's hard. Being there with your presence is enough. Listen well. Be compassionate. Rejoice when they rejoice, weep when they weep (Romans 12:15). Treat your teen with the same kindness you'd want to receive in your own joys and sorrows.

I'm not saying we can't ever offer perspective or advice. We have true wisdom and discernment to share. However, our timing matters. Some days—especially in the midst of fluctuating emotions—our kids just need a hug and for us to sit with them and listen and pray for them. When their emotions are more settled (and they will settle) might be a better time for giving advice. Some teens may appear to reject your presence when they just aren't ready for your advice. Ask the Lord for discernment to know when to speak and when to listen. Pray in the moment. But most of all, be present and available in the joys and the sorrows. Your teen needs you.

Available to Help

We don't always know when our kids will need our help. However, when problems do arise, we want to be that "phone a friend" lifeline they can turn to. If we pack our schedules too full, we won't have the bandwidth to be there for them when they call. Our kids will notice if we treat their presence as an interruption. It takes mental preparedness to be available to them when they ask for help with a class project, math homework, or need a ride to a friend's house. Being available matters.

We may think that we can simply hire out some of these tasks to other people. Or perhaps buy expensive gifts to make up for our lack of availability. However, money doesn't provide relational closeness. In fact, research shows an inverse relationship between income and relational closeness to parents because affluent kids are often aware of their low rank on their parents' priority list.[2] Teen psychologist Levine notes, "Material advantages do not lessen the sting of unavailability."[3]

Our teens need so much more than financial security or extravagant vacations. Don't discount the importance of mundane carpool-ride conversations and reading over English essays. It matters that our teens believe we are available when they need us.

Available to Share (Let Them Know Your Life Too)

Relationships aren't one-sided. Our presence around and with our teen helps them observe that we are people too. We have good days and bad days. We receive hard news and endure disappointments.

Just today, I found out that my mom's cancer has returned. It's not the news I was hoping to hear. When my daughter came home from school, I told her the diagnosis. She lovingly asked me, "Mom, how are you doing?" I didn't hide behind overly positive platitudes. I told her, "It's really sad. I'm concerned and don't want Mimi to have to go through all of these treatments again." She hugged me and let me share about my hard day with her. I was so impressed with her ability to ask good questions and comfort me.

Of course, our teens don't need to know all of our struggles. However, it's good to share our lives with them in age-appropriate ways so that they can learn to share their lives with others. Being part of a family means we share together in the good and bad, laughter and tears.

We can't be available if we are always in a rush. We need family schedules that allow for downtime. Make time together a priority. Enjoy family meals together. Pray together. Ride in the car together. Sit in a room and read books together. Cook meals together. Play games together. As you do so, talk, listen, laugh, and cry. Offer your teens something better than the shallow mirage of community that social media promises. If they've tasted real community, the fake stuff won't be as enticing.

The teen years are an opportunity for our kids to start to get to know us as more than just mom and dad. As you talk with them, don't be afraid to let them know more about your story—the times you failed and the times you succeeded. When one of my kids accidentally hit something with the car, I told all of them about the time I drove through the garage door. Their eyes were wide with disbelief as they all started laughing and asking me tons of questions. It helps them to know we were once teenagers too and made our own share of mistakes.

It's also good for them when we share about bad days or good days that we are currently experiencing. They need to know that adulthood is full of its own ups and downs. Let them be a part of your life, just like you want to be a part of theirs. Invite them to pray for you in the hard times and celebrate with you in the good times. And, when they offer you that hug on a difficult day, enjoy it. Parents need comfort too.

Practical Advice: Living Wisely

In 1543, Copernicus published his seminal work *On the Revolutions of the Heavenly Spheres*, in which he formulated a model of the earth orbiting the sun, rather than vice versa. He had completed the work years earlier, but didn't publish it until he was on his deathbed for fear of the unconventional (and to some, heretical) claims it contained. It changed the world of astronomy and the way we understand the earth's place in the universe.

We now readily accept that the moon rotates around the earth and the earth rotates around the sun. Laws of gravity and mathematics (that are way over my head) have continued to prove the validity of Copernicus's disruptive theory.

These planetary understandings offer a helpful image in my mind when I think about availability in parenting. As parents, we're like the moon, a faithful light in the midst of darkness for our teens. We're there, but we're not actually generating the light—the sun does that. We're simply reflecting a bigger and better light as we shine. We're dependent on the sun's light, and we're not the ones actually generating the warmth. And it's the power of the sun's gravitational pull that keeps the earth on track, not the moon's strength.

As parents, we're limited in what we can do. We are needed, but our power is reflective—we're pointing our teens to someone bigger and better than ourselves. It matters that we're present, but we're unable to always be available—only God is omnipresent. Just as the moon waxes and wanes, our availability changes in different seasons. Only God can fully meet our teen with the promise, "I will not leave you or forsake you" (Joshua 1:5). He's the true light that shines in the darkness. We spend our lives continually pointing our kids to the bigger and better light.

While we've spent this chapter considering the importance of our availability, I want to close with some needed caveats. Our availability is reflective of God's, but it's not God's. While his presence is limitless, ours has limits. We need to consider those realities so that we can live with wisdom (and not guilt) as we parent our teens.

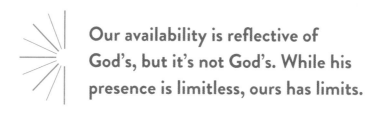

Our availability is reflective of God's, but it's not God's. While his presence is limitless, ours has limits.

Availability with Boundaries (It's Okay to Have Limits)

Being available to our teens doesn't mean that we don't have necessary boundaries on our time. It's okay if you can't drive every carpool and be at every game. Many parents are balancing multiple kids' schedules and their own work schedules. Our presence at one kid's game means we have to miss someone else's flute lesson. Life doesn't always fit into tidy buckets.

We also have limits to our emotional capacities. While some kids will clam up the moment we ask them how they're doing, others may talk on and on and on. It's okay to tell them you'd love to hear more about the story on the way to soccer practice, but you need a few minutes right now to answer some work emails. We want our teens to know that they are important to us, but they're not the center of our universe—only God can be that.

Some teens seem unaware that their parents might have anything else going on in their life other than being their parent. It's okay to say, "I can help you with that assignment in 30 minutes, but right now isn't a good time." Our availability doesn't have to be only when it suits our teen. It's a conversation that's happening in our homes each and every day. I've told my kids that I need them to ask me for help with any "deep thinking" homework before 9:00 p.m. My brain stops being able to process math equations and other complex information later in the evening. It's not that I'm unwilling to help, I just know that I'm no help that late at night.

Having boundaries sets expectations that your teen will take into all of their future relationships. Everyone has strengths and weaknesses. Some people need more sleep than others. Some people have energy that seems to go on for days. Some people can organize quickly and confidently. Others struggle just to clean out the junk drawer. Everyone is dealing with a finite amount of time, resources, and abilities. Our teens need the safety of knowing we are available, alongside the awareness that we have limitations.

Availability with Independence (Have Your Own Life)

It's also important for us to distinguish the difference between availability and over-involvement. We need to be around, but we don't need to be overly fixated on everything our kids are doing. We want to be an available presence, not a controlling one. Kids don't want to be smothered by our presence or involvement.

As a parent, it's important to cultivate interests independent from your teen. Over-involvement doesn't always lead to emotional closeness. Levine notes,

> Parents can be overinvolved and children can still feel isolated. Controlling and overinvolved parents typically leave kids feeling angry or alienated, neither of which is conducive to emotional closeness. And it is emotional closeness, maternal warmth in particular, that is as close as we get to a silver bullet against psychological impairment.[4]

Kids understand the difference between being a warmly welcomed member of the home versus the center of the universe. (And, honestly, it's somewhat overwhelming to be the center of anyone's universe.) They're not able to bear up underneath the pressure. If your teen thinks that your happiness rests on their grades, social standing, appearance, or athletic success, they'll want to avoid talking with you about those topics.

There's a worldly adage that says something like, "You're only as happy as your least happy child." Truthfully, that's a lot of pressure on your teen. Don't let it be true of your parenting. Our joy and happiness need to be rooted in God's love for us, not our teen's performance or happiness. We can ask thoughtful questions, but we want to avoid being an anxious, fretful presence (which is probably rooted in one of our own idols).

As we develop interests apart from our teen, we may find a surprising outcome: We actually become more interesting to them. I've spent years gardening in the backyard. It's simply something I love to do (primarily because eating a fresh ripe tomato is something I really love to do). A few years ago, my teenage son began helping me. He would haul dirt, dig holes, and pull up weeds. Then he decided he wanted to plant some of his own seeds. Now we have corn, carrots, and potatoes growing in garden plots that he created. It's our thing we do together. We talk about what to plant, where to plant, and get excited when we see our gardens growing side by side. Having my own interest ended up providing opportunities for us to spend time together.

I encourage you as a parent: Have your own interests. Find a hobby, go back to school, volunteer, and build friendships. Of course, be thoughtful. Don't busy yourself so much that you miss these years (they will go so very fast). But, at the same time, don't spend your life worrying about every detail of your teens' lives. Be present in your own life as you're actively involved in your teens' lives. It will be a blessing to your teens for them to know you'll be okay when they leave home.

Availability with Expectations: Don't Do for Them What They Can Do for Themselves

Have expectations of your teens. It's a rule to live by: *Don't do for your teen what they can do for themselves.* You're not helping them if you're still packing their lunches, making their beds, checking their homework assignments, and doing their laundry in high school. Our teens want to be treated like adults, and letting them take on the responsibilities of adulthood is important.

I began working full time when my youngest was in middle school. Often, I felt spread thin because there wasn't enough time to do all that needed to be done. My biggest concern about my work was that my family would feel neglected. Over time, I realized that my inability to get everything done on my own was actually a blessing to my kids. They learned to do their own laundry and help with dinner. They did their own homework and managed their own schedules. Their rooms…well, their rooms were a complete mess. Beds weren't made regularly, but at least all of them know how to make a bed. My limitations allowed them to rise to the occasion. They could do a lot more around the home than I was giving them credit for.

As kids learn to do things for themselves, they grow in confidence: "Kids who learn early in life that they're capable of mastering activities that at first feel a little stressful grow up better able to handle stress of all kinds."[5] It's not good for a four-year-old to be making their own dinner—that's probably a sign of neglect. However, it is good for your 14-year-old to try to make dinner. Yes, they'll have questions. They won't know how to manage all the details at first. They will probably overcook the chicken or burn the biscuits. We've all burned something or other in our lives, and I've eaten plenty of tough chicken. It's okay for your teen to feel a little overwhelmed when learning a new task. It's not okay for them to enter adulthood unprepared to take care of themselves.

Be available and have reasonable expectations. Don't write their papers or do their homework or keep checking their grades. Let them do their own laundry and make their own beds. Allow them opportunities to cook a meal. Don't be afraid to let them use an ax or hammer a nail. Be available to help, but don't do the work for them.

I've found that as my kids have grown more independent in these ways, they've actually been more appreciative of my help. When I know they're in a busy season with tests or sports and I offer to fold their clothes for them, they thank me *more* than if I always did their laundry for them. They correctly view taking care of their belongings as their job. So, my help is seen as a welcome gift, not an entitled right.

Having expectations of our teens communicates to them that we know they are competent and able to do the job. Having availability for our teens communicates to them that they are valued and loved. We want to wisely combine both so that our teens can be blessed to be a blessing to others.

A Note of Gospel Hope

As a mom of multiple teens working a full-time job, sometimes I wished that I could be in multiple places all at once. I wanted to see my daughter's soccer game and still make it in time to see my son pitch at baseball. I wanted to say yes to that project at work and be able to help with my daughter's essays for college applications. I wanted to volunteer for my daughter's play and attend Bible study with my friends. It's tough, on a daily basis, to decide between multiple good choices.

Whatever choices you make in this busy season, let me encourage you: Don't neglect your time in the Word and prayer. As we parent teens, we desperately need time to be recharged and refreshed with truth from God's Word. Prayer is our lifeline, and God promises us wisdom as we seek him. He's available and has the power to help guide us when we are unsure about the way forward. Ask him to give you discernment for all the choices before you today.

May the Lord refresh you!

MK

Parenting Principles to Ponder

- We are not alone as parents. God is an ever-present strength in every battle. We can parent with hope because God is with us.

- Have expectations for your teens. This is a rule to live by: *Don't do for your teen what they can do for themselves.*

- Our availability is reflective of God's, but it's not God's. While his presence is limitless, ours has limits.

CHAPTER 9

Affection: A Home of Warmth

I n the thirteenth century, the controversial ruler Frederick II rose to power in Sicily as Holy Roman Emperor. He was excommunicated twice, married three times, and often in armed conflict with other countries. Frederick II was a patron of the sciences and arts and welcomed scholars to his court. However, his desire for knowledge led to multiple unethical and gruesome experiments.

One such experiment was recorded by an Italian Franciscan monk, Salimbene di Adam, in his work *The Twelve Calamities of Emperor Frederick II*. Languages fascinated the emperor, and he wanted to uncover the original language that had been given to Adam and Eve. To do so, he conducted an experiment in which a group of babies were given over to the care of nurses who were instructed to not interact with or talk to the children. They were allowed to feed and bathe them, but they were not allowed to speak or offer them comfort of any kind. By removing conversation, Frederick thought he would uncover the original language of humans.

However, he uncovered something shockingly different. All of the children in the experiment died. One historian explained, "The children, starved of any form of affection, warmth and basic interaction, died, quite simply, of a lack of love."[1]

Similarly, in the 1940s, Austrian psychoanalyst René Spitz proposed the theory that infants in institutions suffered from sickness and death more often because of a lack of loving caregiving. He tested his theory by studying one group of infants raised in isolated hospital cribs with those raised in prison with their incarcerated mothers. Of the two groups, the statistics were shocking. Thirty-seven percent of the infants in the hospital wards died, while all the children raised in prison with their mothers lived.[2] Once again, parental love made a huge impact on the physical and emotional well-being of the child. Since then, study after study has concluded that food, clothing, and basic caregiving are not enough. Children need love.

Our teens need parental love. **There's no stronger foundation; there's no bigger blessing.**

In an unexpected way, perhaps Frederick did uncover the language of all languages. God is love (1 John 4:16), and God's love spoke the world into existence. Whatever verbal language we may speak, we all understand the lovingkindness of a hug or a tender grasp of a hand or tears of sympathy. We know that while faith, hope, and love remain, the greatest of these is love (1 Corinthians 13:13). Love is the language that allows babies to survive, and it is the foundation that helps our teens to thrive.

I've saved this for the final chapter, but there's nothing more important to say in this book than this: *Our teens need parental love.* There's no stronger foundation; there's no bigger blessing. Love is like a force field of protection around our teens. We don't outgrow our need for love. In fact, research has shown that the more connected you are to others, the less risk you have of dying at any age.[3]

There's no such thing as too much love, only misguided notions of what it means to be loving. That's why we need God's Word to guide us. We'll spend this chapter digging into how God expressed his love for us, and how that directs us as parents. We'll consider purposeful ways we can lovingly engage with our teens, as well as think through what it means to be an affectionate parent. We'll conclude by considering some practical ways we can create homes filled with warmth and laughter, with hopeful enjoyment during these special years with our teens.

There's no such thing as too much love, only misguided notions of what it means to be loving.

Principles for Parents: Thinking Biblically

When Jesus was asked, "Which commandment is the most important?" he replied, "'You shall love the Lord your God with all your heart and with all your soul and with all your mind and with all your strength.' The second is this: 'You shall love your neighbor as yourself.' There is no other commandment greater than these" (Mark 12:30-31).

It's interesting that both of these commandments begin with "You shall love." First, we are to love God, and then we are to love others. Our affections matter. And God defines what it means to be loving. Time and again, Scripture clarifies, *This is what it means to be loving*. Let's begin with what it means for us to love God.

Loving God

How do we know if we love God? Thankfully, this is not measured by our day-to-day feelings or the emotional high we experienced at a summer camp. Jesus told his disciples, "If you love me, you will keep my commandments" (John 14:15). In one of his letters to Christians, the apostle John clarified even further, "By this we know that we love the children of God, when we love God and obey his commandments. For this is the love of God, that we keep his commandments. And his commandments are not burdensome" (1 John 5:2-3).

Here's what this passage tells us: *Our love for God is displayed in our obedience to his commands.* In a similar way, our love for others is displayed in our love for God and our obedience to his commands. If I'm not walking in obedience to God, then I'm not loving God or my neighbor.

Sometimes we spend so much time trying to think of amazing or imaginative ways to demonstrate love to the people in our lives. We conceive of special gifts, trips, words of affirmation, amazing acts of service, or special experiences. Have you ever considered that the best way to show love to your children, your spouse, your co-workers, your neighbor, your city, and the world is to love God and obey him? It's that simple and that difficult all at the same time. However, it's what we were made to do: walk as Jesus walked. That's how we love others. And we have the promise that his commands are not burdensome. With the help of the Spirit, we can joyfully walk in the freedom of obedience.

As we think about our relationship with God, it's important to remember that our obedience *displays* our love for God, but it doesn't *earn* God's love for us. As the apostle Paul wrote, "God shows his love for us in that while we were still sinners, Christ died for us" (Romans 5:8). God's love for us is independent of our performance and based on Christ's work done on our behalf. Therefore, we can claim the promise, "The steadfast love of the Lord never ceases; his mercies never come to an end" (Lamentations 3:22). Fully cleansed by Christ, we have no fear of losing God's favor.

Loving our teen begins by loving God with all our heart, soul, mind, and strength. If our affections are misplaced or out of order, we'll find ourselves mired in fearfulness, anxiety, and idolatry in our parenting. Instead, we want to parent with hope that flows from love. Our faithful example matters to our teens. *Handing Down the Faith* explains:

> Some readers might be surprised to know that the single, most powerful causal influence on the religious lives of American teenagers and young adults is the religious lives of their parents. Not their peers, not the media, not their youth group leaders or clergy, not their religious school teachers. Myriad studies show that, beyond a doubt, the parents of American youth play *the* leading role in shaping the character of their religious and spiritual lives, even well after they leave the home.[4]

That's pretty surprising, isn't it? And perhaps somewhat sobering—parents play the leading role in shaping thier children's spiritual lives. Rather than fear the culture or fret about the latest social media app, we're called to be parents who put all our efforts into loving God and walking by faith. That's where we begin. Our hope in God, our love for God, and our obedience to God makes a profound impact on our teens. Too often, we put aside our relationship with God and think that we are loving our children by putting them first. However, when we prioritize our teens over God, we are actually failing to love them as we should.

Our hope in God, our love for God, and our obedience to God makes a profound impact on our teens.

One sobering example of misplaced priorities is found in the book of 1 Samuel. We are told the tales of two parents, with two very different outcomes. In the first two chapters, we read of the story of Hannah, a woman disheartened and discouraged. Year after year she prayed for a child, desperately hoping to have a baby. Year after year she remained barren. Out of anguish, Hannah prayed, "O Lord of hosts, if you will indeed look on the affliction of your servant and remember me and not forget your servant, but will give to your servant a son, then I will give him to the Lord all the days of his life" (1 Samuel 1:11).

Seeing her deep distress (and mistaking it for drunkenness), Eli the priest approached her. Upon hearing her story, Eli promised, "Go in peace, and the God of Israel grant your petition that you have made to him" (1 Samuel 1:17). Hannah dried her tears and returned home. Soon she found out that she was pregnant, and when she gave birth to a son, she named him Samuel. After he was weaned, she took Samuel to Eli and offered him to the Lord to fulfill her vow. Her tears gave way to praise as she dedicated her son to God. Hannah's love for the Lord overflowed in sacrificial obedience. She gave her son back to him, honoring the vow she had made.

In contrast to Hannah's wholehearted obedience, we read the story of Eli and his sons. We're told, "Now the sons of Eli were worthless men. They did not know the Lord" (1 Samuel 2:12). They disobeyed God's regulations in worship and committed sexual immorality with women who came to the temple. Even though Eli warned them, they did not listen, but continued to sin before the Lord. Eventually a man of God came to Eli, confronting him with his wrongdoing: "Why then do you scorn my sacrifices and my offerings that I commanded for my dwelling, and *honor your sons above me* by fattening yourselves on the choicest parts of every offering of my people Israel?" (1 Samuel 2:29, emphasis added).

Notice that God confronted Eli about his affections toward his sons. Eli wrongly honored his sons above God. His misguided priorities led to all sorts of sin and immorality. Eventually Eli and his sons were killed in judgment for their actions. Who, then, was left as priest for Israel?

Samuel. The boy whose mother entrusted him to God.

He would grow to be the priest who would faithfully lead Israel and speak the Word of God to the people. Hannah gave up her son in obedience to God, and he was a blessing for Israel. Eli honored his sons above God, and they did evil in the sight of God and harm to their neighbors. While it may seem like a good thing to love our children more than anything else, we want to make sure we honor God above all else. We love others best when we love God first. All our other loves will flow from rightly ordered affections.

We love others best when we love God first.

Loving Others

It might seem like the most natural thing to love our children. Of course we love them! However, as our nearest neighbors, sometimes we forget to demonstrate our love by the way we live—especially with our teens. When we live together as a family, there's the reality of proximity. We're in each other's business. My sin affects the lives of those around me, and their sins affect me.

In the daily rush to get from one activity to the next, it's easy to take one another for granted. Often, we're the most short-tempered with the people we are closest to. Our teens might be polite and easygoing around their teachers, but be grumpy and angry when they arrive home because we forgot something as insignificant as picking up their favorite snack at the grocery store.

Part of our task as parents of teens is to model what love looks like up close. We want to create a home environment that proclaims, "I see you. I see all of you—the good, the bad, and the ugly. I even smell you. And you know what? I love you. I delight in you. I want you around." All of us need this kind of unconditional love and support. We get to shower it on our teens (who need it so desperately) just as it's been richly lavished on us in Christ. Rather than let proximity be a reason for short tempers and annoyance, we want to communicate a deep love and acceptance. We want love to be the air we breathe in our homes. So, let's consider what that love looks like as we engage with our teens on a daily basis.

Purposeful Parenting: Engaging Gracefully

Some days, our teens can be tough to love. They can be grumpy and moody and their insecurities can overflow in bursts of anger that are most often directed our way. It's now more than ever that they need our unconditional love and support. We can (and should) have expectations about their behavior and consequences for misbehavior. However, don't let words rashly spoken in a teenage fit undermine your warmth. Don't turn cold when they get hot under the collar. Be careful to avoid withholding affection.

When your teens makes straight *A*'s and obey curfew, give them affection. When they sneak out and make poor choices, give them affection. When they're insecure and anxious, give them affection. Whatever they do, let them know you love them. Don't condition your love on their behavior. A lack of affection is never a good consequence for a lack in behavior. Firmly correct and kindly rebuke, but always demonstrate love. Lavish love upon your teen like you slather sunscreen on a small child. Your love is the best barrier for the world's damaging rays.

Love Sacrifices

The Bible tells the greatest love story that's ever been told. Jesus came to rescue his bride (the church) from the power of the enemy (the devil). How did he win his bride? Even though he was rejected, he gave his life to pay her debt. He sacrificed everything so she could be free. His sacrificial love is our example.

We may want accolades and words of thanks from our teens. We may want clean rooms and neatly folded clothing put away in drawers. We may want kids who work hard at school. We may want kids who love going to church, read their Bibles daily, and tell us the truth. We may want kids who love to eat their vegetables. These are all good things.

Most likely, however, our teens won't live up to our expectations. As parents, it's vital to understand the difference between our personal preferences and God's commands. Don't force or demand your teens to do everything your way. Wait patiently. Prioritize your relationships with them over your personal preferences. Hold your tongue and humbly receive critique. Don't expect them to meet your needs, but be willing to lay down your life in sacrifice: "By this we know love, that he laid down his life for us, and we ought to lay down our lives for the brothers…Little children, let us not love in word or talk but in deed and in truth" (1 John 3:16-18).

Looking back, I realize how many ways my dad sacrificed his personal comforts for our family. In high school, I drove a nicer car than he did because he wanted me to be safe (it was a used Honda Accord, so it wasn't a luxury vehicle, but it was safe!). He always paid for everything he could to provide, and never complained. I never felt like a burden. He made me feel loved and protected. He sacrificed to take care of us. I regularly heard the words "I love you" and witnessed his words lived out in humble and sacrificial ways.

Keep serving, keep sacrificing, keep loving. Like a sculptor who slowly chips away to create a masterpiece, love takes time to uncover the beauty of its slow work on a soul.

Do your teens experience you actively sacrificing for them, or do they feel a heavy weight from your expectations? I'm not saying to *tell* them all the sacrifices you are making for them. It's not helpful to parent with self-focused language like, "Don't you know all that I've done for you?" Instead, display sacrificial love to them, day in and day out. Let them experience it, without fanfare or attention. The Lord sees and knows. Eventually, your teens may notice and thank you. But don't have big expectations in this season. Rather, keep serving, keep sacrificing, keep loving. Like a sculptor who slowly chips away to create a masterpiece, love takes time to uncover the beauty of its slow work on a soul. Take the long view of parenting. This season is only one part of the journey.

Love Acts

We often hear the words in 1 Corinthians 13 read at weddings as describing the ultimate example of romantic love. The passage pictures how people in the church are to love one another, and those affections begin in the home. I know the words are familiar, but take a moment to slowly read them again with me:

> Love is patient and kind; love does not envy or boast; it is not arrogant or rude. It does not insist on its own way; it is not irritable or resentful; it does not rejoice at wrongdoing, but rejoices with the truth. Love bears all things, believes all things, hopes all things, endures all things (1 Corinthians 13:4-7).

Love is a feeling, but it's not only a feeling. Love acts lovingly toward others. Demonstrating love is a deliberate choice we make in spite of how we feel on any given day. You may feel tired and irritable, but love chooses to be patient and kind. You may feel frustrated and overwhelmed by your teen's poor choices, but love chooses to bear with them without resentment or arrogance. You may prefer a certain order in your home or hairstyle or food choices, but love does not insist on its own way. Love acts with the other person's best in mind.

Love Corrects

As parents, our love for our teens means we believe God's Word is best for them. Part of rejoicing with the truth means correcting wrongdoing. Unconditional love isn't in opposition to discipline. In fact, we're told the opposite. Jesus wrote (through the apostle John) to the church in Laodicea, "Those whom I love, I reprove and discipline, so be zealous and repent" (Revelation 3:19). Paul confronted the Corinthians because he loved them: "I wrote to you out of much affliction and anguish of heart and with many tears, not to cause you pain but to let you know the abundant love that I have for you" (2 Corinthians 2:4).

When our teens disobey God's Word (which is different than not liking our preferences), they need our loving correction. They also need a listening ear. Some of our teens may be fighting sin and feeling trapped. They may keep going back to pornography or gossip or lying or drinking and feel deeply ashamed. Discipline during the teen years is not a one-size-fits-all tool. Helping your teens make right choices takes wisdom, prayer, and conversations with them. One teen may need your help finding software to keep them from sin, another teen might need your advice on how to apologize to a friend for an unkind word or deed.

Other teens may not be fighting sin at all. Perhaps unbelief sits below whatever sin is rising to the surface. If your teen isn't a Christian or doesn't claim to believe, that doesn't mean you can't have expectations for behavior in your household, but it does mean your conversations take on a different focus. We want our teens to obey from inner faith. If they don't believe, keep having conversations about the good news. Ask questions, listen to their doubts, help them find answers, and pray that the Spirit would awaken them to faith. Be concerned about how their sin reflects the condition of their soul, not how it affects other people's opinions about your parenting.

As you correct, avoid being critical in spirit. A word of correction is rooted in God's wisdom, but a critical spirit is rooted in pride that wants our teen to do things *our* way. That may work when our children are younger, but nitpicking every last thing is going to exasperate your teen. None of us wants to be followed around all day being told all the things we didn't do well enough: *Tuck in your shirt. Are you really wearing that? Why didn't you study more for that test? Comb your hair. Don't eat that; it's junk!* Imagine having an overly critical boss who is never pleased—that would be exhausting. Rome wasn't built in a day, and neither are people. Be patient and realize you don't have to correct everything in this season.

Avoiding a critical spirit takes discernment. Choose the battles that really matter. It's just not that important if your teen gets a bad grade on a quiz or if their clothing doesn't match or if they haven't taken a shower in a week. Don't let small battles distract you from your primary goal. Eventually they will mature in these areas—just as they outgrew two-year-old tantrums. Correct sinful attitudes and behaviors, but don't be a critical parent.

Love Delights

Instead of being critical, delight in your teen. Our teens are living in a world where they're judged daily for their appearance, intelligence, likability, and social media savvy. It's exhausting for them. Gift your teen with the warmth of your delight. Zephaniah talks about the Lord's love for us: "The Lord your God is in your midst, a mighty one who will save; he will rejoice over you with gladness; he will quiet you by his love; he will exult over you with loud singing" (Zephaniah 3:17). I love this fatherly picture of God rejoicing over his children with gladness. Be that kind of parent.

I'll never forget one of the best pieces of advice I ever received as a mom—and it came from the *Oprah Winfrey Show*. (Don't stop reading; it's good advice!) Oprah was interviewing Toni Morrison, and I'll never forget what Toni said about parenting. With the wisdom of a sage, she looked at the camera as though she was speaking to my soul:

> When a kid walks in the room, your child or anyone else's child, *does your face light up?* That's what they're looking for. When my children used to walk in the room when they were little, I looked at them to see if they had buckled their trousers or if their hair was combed or if their socks were up. You think your affection and your deep love is on display because you are caring for them. It's not. When they see you, they see the critical face, "What's wrong now?"…Let your face speak what's in your heart.[5]

Does your face light up when your teen walks in the room?

It's a simple act of love. But so often we miss profound opportunities to delight in our children. Morrison's words reminded me of Zephaniah's understanding of God's fatherly love and the importance of small actions that greatly bless our children. We don't want our teens to feel like we're constantly watching them with a critical eye; we want them to know we see them with a loving heart.

When your teen walks in the room, look at them. See them. Thank God that they are in your life and in your home. Greet them with a smile, not a sigh. Let them know they are more important than your work, your phone, your dinner preparation. The warmth of your greeting matters—light up with affection.

Practical Advice: Living Wisely

Practically, how can these truths make a difference? As we center our lives on God's love, we're changed as parents. We build homes of affection with different tools. We need warmth, consideration, and hope.

A Home of Warmth

Life is hard, the world is cold, but we have the opportunity for the light of the gospel to burn brightly in our homes. A home filled with warmth is an environment we all want to create. Being able to laugh at ourselves—and not take ourselves too seriously—is a great place to begin. Homes of warmth allow for disagreement and discussion, patiently listening to one another with respect. Warm homes invite praise and cheering one another on in success, as well as offering one another sympathy in sadness. Both are important.

Welcoming homes don't only celebrate wins. They offer the warmth of comfort when you don't make the team, fail a test, or get in a fender bender at school. Love covers an offense (Proverbs 17:9) and doesn't keep records of wrongs (1 Corinthians 13:5 NIV). In warm homes, each person accepts each and every other person just because they are part of the family, not because they are perfect.

We want to do whatever we can to be winsome and wise, compassionate and kind. The environment in our homes matters. Overly rigid homes can feel suffocating instead of inviting. If your teen doesn't like to be at your house, it's good to ask them why. Listen carefully and be open to their perspective. You may be able to make small changes that have a big impact.

In homes filled with warmth, family members have fun together. And that looks different for every family. Some families laugh around board games or charades. Others enjoy being outdoors. Some love to travel together or dance the night away together. I walked into our den one Christmas afternoon and laughed to see everyone lounging together by the fire reading a new book. That may not be your family's idea of fun, but it's ours (we admit to being rather boring). You don't have to do what other families are doing. In fact, it might make you all miserable to follow some Instagram influencer's version of a perfect outing with your family. Be unique, be together, and build a home that's full of warmth and love for one another.

Also, take the time to laugh together. Let humor be a regular part of your interactions. Be able to laugh at yourself and be silly. For years, my kids have kept a quote book of funny family statements. We read them regularly and belly laugh at the things that have been said. Laughter bonds a family together in a special way.

A Home of Consideration

One book that greatly impacted my understanding of love was Gary Chapman's *The Five Love Languages.* If you haven't read it, I highly recommend it. In the book, he shares five different ways people give and receive love: quality time, words of affection, acts of service, physical touch, and gifts. His basic premise is that people are different in the ways they want to show love and the ways they experience love.

Most of us have a couple of primary ways we receive love. Our teens are similar. Some teens may beam after a word of affirmation. Others may love receiving gifts. Some teens may want quality time or a physical touch, while other teens might experience your affection because you cleaned their room for them. Every teen is different and experiences love differently.

As you think about your teen, consider what makes them feel loved. Don't diminish the way they receive love if it's different from the way you receive love. You may not be a hugger, but your teen might need a hug. You may not care about gifts, but that might be what makes your teen feel noticed. You may want to teach responsibility, but you can also do acts of service. If I'm loving other people based solely on how I want to be loved, I'm showing me-centered love. Love unselfishly considers what makes another person feel loved.

If your teen is going through a difficult season, it's particularly helpful to know the best way to express your love to them. Some teens feel unlovable or unworthy of love because of past choices. Or they may feel criticized day after day. Or perhaps school is difficult, and they struggle every day to keep up with everyone else. In such times, our teens desperately need us to come to them with every tool we've got to show how much we care for them.

Teens can sense whether you find them annoying, difficult, or exasperating. While you may feel all those things, you don't have to express those emotions to your teen (instead, talk to a friend, a counselor, or a prayer group). As parents, we choose to *be* loving, even when we may want to pull all our hair out in frustration. Honoring your teen above yourself is an outworking of love, as Paul explains: "Love must be sincere. Hate what is evil; cling to what is good. Be devoted to one another in love. Honor one another above yourselves" (Romans 12:9-10 NIV).

A Home of Hope

Sometimes I watch the news and find myself deeply concerned about the state of the world. There are wars and rumors of wars. There's violence, cynicism, disunity, ungodliness, and evil masquerading as good. Paul warned Timothy, "Understand this, that in the last days there will come times of difficulty. For people will be lovers of self, lovers of money, proud, arrogant, abusive, disobedient to their parents, ungrateful, unholy, heartless, unappeasable, slanderous, without self-control, brutal, not loving good, treacherous, reckless, swollen with conceit, lovers of pleasure rather than lovers of God, having the appearance of godliness, but denying its power" (2 Timothy 3:1-5). He wrote that almost 2,000 years ago, but it sounds like he's describing my news feed.

How do we parent in a world that's heartless, unappeasable, and without self-control? What hope can we offer our teens? How can we avoid being fearful, anxious, and worried all the time?

Paul continued,

> As for you, continue in what you have learned and have firmly believed, knowing from whom you learned it and how from childhood you have been acquainted with the sacred writings, which are able to make you wise for salvation through faith in Christ Jesus. All Scripture is breathed out by God and profitable for teaching, for reproof, for correction, and for training in

righteousness, that the man of God may be complete, equipped for every good work (2 Timothy 3:14-17).

Paul was not fretful about what was happening. He was steadfast. Immovable. Abounding in the work of the Lord. He tells us that when it looks like chaos reigns, we know how the story ends. Calmly and purposefully, he points us back to the Word. It's the anchor we need, holding us fast in the midst of life's storms.

Like Paul, we began with the Word, and we end with the Word. Jesus is the Word made flesh, and his words are life-giving and hope-filling. Where do we turn as parents to transform our fear into faith and apprehension into expectation? How do we best love our teenagers? We steadfastly continue in what we've learned. We faithfully share what will make our teens wise for salvation. We let the Word do the work. It can equip our children with eternal truth for whatever new philosophy or agenda is around the next corner. We're hopeful because truth doesn't change, even when culture does. Even though we're powerless to awaken our teen's heart, we're hopeful because the Spirit can.

As we live in light of what we believe, we parent differently than the world around us. We don't feel like we have to take control because we know God is in control. We don't focus on earthly success because we know eternal blessings await. We don't despair in a world that's full of trouble because we know Jesus has overcome the world (John 16:33). We listen to Jesus and we live for Jesus. We love our teens and tell them about Jesus. Over and over in a thousand different ways, we share the gospel with them.

The word *gospel* literally means "good news." In the ancient world, a herald would be sent ahead of a victorious army, proclaiming the "gospel"—that the war was won and peace established. Even though people may not yet be experiencing the fruit of victory, they rejoiced in knowing it was coming. In a similar way, we parent with hope because we know the victory has been won. We live in the shadow of death, but the enemy of enemies (death) has been defeated. One day, every tear will be dried and sorrow and sighing will flee away (Isaiah 51:11). We walk with calm confidence today because our future is secure.

This good news enables us to be loving parents. The gospel pardons us from past sin and it empowers us for present holiness. We're freed from self-preoccupation, worry, and fear. We're calm, confident, and courageous. We walk by *faith* in Christ. We live with *hope* in the Spirit's work. We parent with *love* by the Father's example.

> So now faith, hope, and love abide, these three;
> but the greatest of these is love
> (1 Corinthians 13:13).

A Note of Gospel Hope

It's hard to believe we're at the end of this book. I wish we could sit down for lunch or for coffee and you could tell me about your teens. I'd love to hear about the joys you're experiencing, as well as discuss the struggles you're facing. Whatever you are going through today, I'm praying from 2 Chronicles 20. There, we read the story of King Jehoshaphat. He was warned of a great multitude that was coming against Israel, ready to do battle. Jehoshaphat was afraid and sought the Lord. Recognizing his helplessness, he prayed, "O our God…we are powerless against this great horde that is coming against us. We do not know what to do, but our eyes are on you" (2 Chronicles 20:12). Whatever we are facing as parents, this can be our prayer: *We don't know what to do, but our eyes are on you.*

God met Jehoshaphat's prayer with these words of encouragement: "'You will not need to fight in this battle. Stand firm, hold your position, and see the salvation of the Lord on your behalf, O Judah and Jerusalem.' Do not be afraid and do not be dismayed…the Lord will be with you" (2 Chronicles 20:17). Without God, we have every reason to be fearful and fretful. With God, we can parent with hope, raising teens for Christ in a secular culture. We have his promises, his power, and his presence. Stand firm, hold your position, and may you see the salvation of the Lord on your behalf.

Praying with hope,

MK

Parenting Principles to Ponder

- Loving our teen begins by loving God with all our heart, soul, mind, and strength. If our affections are misplaced or out of order, we'll find ourselves mired in fearfulness, anxiety, and idolatry in our parenting.

- Whatever your teen does, let them know you love them. Don't condition your love on their behavior. A lack of affection is never a good consequence for a lack in behavior. Firmly correct and kindly rebuke, but always love.

- Homes of warmth allow for disagreement and discussion, patiently listening to one another with respect.

A Secure Place
for Hope

This book has been the hardest one I've written. I've labored over these words, hoping they will be helpful. I've read a ton of books for research. I've talked to older parents and people currently raising teens. I've prayed for wisdom and insight.

However, I don't write from an ivory tower of perfect parenting. I've made plenty of mistakes, with bumps and bruises along the way. I know there's so much I don't know. Every parenting situation is so complex, and each teen so unique in their responses. I've tried to share general principles alongside practical applications.

I write in the midst of walking with friends who wake up every morning carrying huge parenting burdens. A friend texted me yesterday, distraught because her son's anger exploded in physical ways. Another friend is navigating caring for a teen who is cutting herself and battling suicidal ideation. Another friend's teen is suffering from depression. Another friend's teen is struggling with an eating disorder. Another friend's teen is suffering from anxiety. Another friend recently told me about her son's addiction to porn. Another teen is addicted to video games and another to drugs. Another friend's son is questioning the faith and doesn't know whether

Jesus is worth following. These are all people I know. They are wonderful and loving parents. We're walking together in the reality of addiction, sexual immorality, depression, unbelief, and fear of the future. There are no easy answers.

And yet, in the midst of unsettling realities, there's still hope. It may be a flicker of light some days. But it's there because God is there. He's the anchor in the storm. He's the manna in the wilderness. He's the guiding light in the darkness. We may not understand, we may not get the answers we long for, but we can trust God because he's proven he's worthy of our faith. The worst evil (the cross) purchased our greatest good (our salvation). God can use the broken paths of these teen years. Those who walk with God often experience winding, perplexing, and unexpected journeys of faith (just think of Abraham, Jacob, Moses, Hannah, Ruth, and David).

Today, we see only one part of the story.

We parent with hope not because everything is easy or understandable. We parent with hope because God is at work in everything that is happening. Our teens are at the beginning of their faith journey. These years are just part of their story. We don't know how all the twists and turns will come together. But we are profoundly blessed to get to be along for the ride.

We parent with hope not because everything is easy or understandable. We parent with hope because God is at work in everything that is happening.

I encourage you: Be thankful for these years. There are so many good moments to enjoy. Your teens are growing spiritually, emotionally, and mentally. You get to have interesting conversations about books, movies, poetry, sports, and faith. You can still take a vacation with everyone there (and everyone can pack for themselves). You can play board games and go on hikes and eat meals together. I've seen so many teens flourishing in their faith, enjoying family time, helping around the home, and growing into such fascinating young adults. The teen years are a unique time to sit back and watch who God is creating your child to be.

Savor these years, the good and the hard. They go so quickly. Soon, your children will be off, setting a course for their own lives. These years are an opportunity to walk with them in the high highs and low lows, communicating to your teens, "No matter what happens, I'm here for you." Focus on your relationships with your teens. Let them know day in and day out how much you love them.

Just like you tell your children not to swim alone, I encourage you, don't do these parenting years alone. We need one another. It's helpful to read parenting books (thank you for reading this one!), but we all need people who can observe our parenting and provide insights into our blind spots. We all have them. Some parents need to loosen up and others need to tighten the reins. This book can provide general principles, but people in your congregation can offer specific feedback. I encourage you to seek out older parents whom you can ask for advice, guidance, wisdom, and prayer.

If you will bear with me one last time (because I know I've said this over and over again), let me encourage you: *Have conversations with your teens.* Listen to their opinions. Learn from their perspectives. Ask good questions. Whatever you do during these years, *remember the relationship*. Don't major on the minors. Keep a healthy perspective by asking yourself, *Will this issue matter in five years?* Whatever you do, be on your knees. "Lord, help me!" is always a good place to begin.

Parenting with hope isn't some type of nebulous positivity or "thinking good thoughts." The object of our hope matters. We parent in light of Peter's exhortation, "Therefore, preparing your minds for action, and being sober-minded, set your hope fully on the grace that will be brought to you at the revelation of Jesus Christ" (1 Peter 1:13).

Hope is like a priceless vase. You don't just set it anywhere. You put it somewhere safe. And there's only one place secure enough as we parent our teens: Set your hope on Jesus. His grace. His goodness. His sovereignty. His power. His love. He can do immeasurably more than you ask or imagine. Rest in him and rely on him.

Jesus is the reason we can parent with hope.

Notes

Chapter 1—An Instruction Manual for Life: God's Word

1. Christian Smith and Amy Adamczyk, *Handing Down the Faith: How Parents Pass Their Religion On to the Next Generation* (New York: Oxford University Press, 2021), 6.

2. John Angell James, *Female Piety* (Morgan, PA: Soli Deo Gloria Publications, 1995), 339.

3. Smith and Adamczyk, *Handing Down the Faith*, 45.

4. Smith and Adamczyk, *Handing Down the Faith*, 5.

5. Smith and Adamczyk, *Handing Down the Faith*, 45.

6. Pamela Li, "4 Types of Parenting Styles and Their Effects on Children," *parenting for brain*, May 11, 2023, https://www.parentingforbrain.com/4-baumrind-parenting-styles/.

7. Smith and Adamczyk, *Handing Down the Faith*, 48.

Chapter 2—The Power of His Presence: Prayer

1. Timothy Keller, *Prayer: Experiencing Awe and Intimacy with God* (New York: Dutton, 2014), 68.

2. Thomas Watson, "The Art of Divine Contentment," *Monergism.com*, https://www.monergism.com/thethreshold/sdg/watson/The%20Art%20of%20Divine%20Contentment%20-%20Thomas%20Watson.pdf (section: Divine Motives to Contentment).

3. Emma Kruger, as cited in Melissa B. Kruger, *5 Things to Pray for Your Kids* (London: The Good Book Company, 2019), 7-8.

Chapter 3—Our Home Away from Home: The Church

1. Emma Kruger, "Considering Attending a Secular University, *The Gospel Coalition*, March 11, 2021, https://www.thegospelcoalition.org/article/consider-secular-university/.

2. Christian Smith and Amy Adamczyk, *Handing Down the Faith: How Parents Pass Their Religion on to the Next Generation* (New York: Oxford University Press, 2021), 6.

3. Jean M. Twenge et al., "Worldwide increases in adolescent loneliness," *Journal of Adolescence*, December 2021, https://www.sciencedirect.com/science/article/pii/S0140197121000853.

4. Derek Thompson, "Why American Teens Are So Sad," *The Atlantic*, April 11, 2022, https://www.theatlantic.com/newsletters/archive/2022/04/american-teens-sadness-depression-anxiety/629524/.

5. "Religious upbringing linked to better health and well-being during early adulthood," *Harvard T.H. Chan School of Public Health*, September 13, 2018, https://www.hsph.harvard.edu/news/press-releases/religious-upbringing-adult-health/.

6. "Religious upbringing linked to better health and well-being during early adulthood."

7. I highly recommend my husband's book, *Surviving Religion 101: Letters to a Christian Student on Keeping the Faith in College* (Wheaton, IL: Crossway, 2021) for older teens and college students dealing with doubt. Another excellent resource for younger teens is Rebecca McLaughlin's *10 Questions Every Teen Should Ask (and Answer) About Christianity* (Wheaton, IL: Crossway, 2021).

Part 2 Introduction

1. Timothy Keller, *Counterfeit Gods: The Empty Promises of Money, Sex, and Power, and the Only Hope That Matters* (New York: Penguin Group, 2009), xvii.

2. John Calvin, *The Institutes of the Christian Religion* (Grand Rapids, MI: Christian Classics Ethereal Library, n.d.), Book 1, chapter 11, section 8, https://www.ccel.org/ccel/c/calvin/institutes/cache/institutes.pdf.

3. Keller, *Counterfeit Gods*, 64.

4. I was helped in these explanations of source idols by a chart from Stephen Speaks shared on the blog of Caleb Cangelosi for Pear Orchard Presbyterian Church, PCA, https://www.pearorchard.org/notes-from-the-orchard-church-blog/2018/11/27/where-do-you-find-yourself-on-this-idolatry-chart (accessed August 13, 2022).

Chapter 4—The Secret of True Success: (Isn't) Scholarship and Affluence

1. Madeline Levine, *The Price of Privilege* (New York: HarperCollins, 2006), 28.

2. Levine, *The Price of Privilege*, 65.

3. Frances E. Jensen, *The Teenage Brain: A Neuroscientist's Survival Guide to Raising Adolescents and Young Adults* (New York: HarperCollins), 80.

4. Levine, *The Price of Privilege*, 79.

5. "Speaking of Psychology: The mental price of affluence, with Suniya Luther, PhD," *American Psychological Association*, https://www.apa.org/news/podcasts/speaking-of-psychology/affluence.

6. Levine, *The Price of Privilege*, 49.

Chapter 5—Beware of Busyness: Sports and Activities

1. Sarah O'Brien, "Americans spend $56 billion on sporting events, *CNBC*, September 11, 2017, https://www.cnbc.com/2017/09/11/americans-spend-56-billion-on-sporting-events.html.

2. "Report: 1 in 4 Americans Watch 5+ Hours of Sports Weekly," *WegENT*, March 24, 2022, https://wegrynenterprises.com/2022/03/24/report-1-in-4-americans-watch-5-hours-of-sports-weekly/.

3. "The Rising Human Cost of Sports Betting," *The New York Times*, January 31, 2022, https://www .nytimes.com/2022/01/31/sports/football/super-bowl-sports-betting.html.

4. David Epstein, *Range: Why Gerneralists Triumph in a Specialized World* (New York: Penguin Random House, 2019), 70.

5. Epstein, *Range*, 7.

6. Frances E. Jensen, *The Teenage Brain: A Neuroscientist's Survival Guide to Raising Adolescents and Young Adults* (New York: HarperCollins, 2016), 89.

7. Jensen, *The Teenage Brain*, 96.

8. Ruthann Richter, "Among teens, sleep deprivation an epidemic," *Stanford Medicine*, October 8, 2015, https://med.stanford.edu/news/all-news/2015/10/among-teens-sleep-deprivation-an-epidemic.html.

9. "NCAA Recruiting Facts," *NCAA*, https://www.nfhs.org/media/886012/recruiting-fact-sheet-web.pdf.

10. "Poll: Three in four adults played sports when they were younger, but only one in four still play," *Harvard T.H. Chan School of Public Health*, June 15, 2015, https://www.hsph.harvard.edu/news/ press-releases/poll-many-adults-played-sports-when-young-but-few-still-play/.

11. Madeline Levine, *The Price of Privilege* (New York: HarperCollins, 2006), 33.

Chapter 6—The Pitfalls of Popularity: Social Acceptance

1. Madeline Levine, *The Price of Privilege* (New York: HarperCollins, 2006), 34.

2. One of my favorite talks on this subject was given by author Jen Wilkin, entitled "Raising an Alien Child" at The Gospel Coalition's National Women's Conference. She presented six areas in which to help our children follow the call to live as aliens and strangers in ways that might make our children stand out rather than easily fit in with the culture around them. If you haven't listened to it, I highly recommend it (meaning, go ahead and listen to it right now).

3. Jean M. Twenge, *iGen: Why Today's Super-Connected Kids Are Growing Up Less Rebellious, More Tolerant, Less Happy—and Completely Unprepared for Adulthood* (New York: Atria, 2017), 39.

4. Twenge, *iGen*, 47.

5. Twenge, *iGen*, 104.

6. Jon Haidt, "The Case for Phone-Free Schools," *After Babel*, June 6, 2023, https://jonathanhaidt .substack.com/p/the-case-for-phone-free-schools?utm_campaign=post&utm_medium=web.

7. Frances E. Jensen, *The Teenage Brain: A Neuroscientist's Survival Guide to Raising Adolescents and Young Adults* (New York: HarperCollins, 2016), 117.

8. Twenge, *iGen*, 77-78.

9. Twenge, *iGen*, 80.

10. Twenge, *iGen*, 82.

11. Twenge, *iGen*, 104.

12. Twenge, *iGen*, 84, 87.

13. Matt Fradd, "10 Shocking Stats about Teens and Pornography," *Covenant Eyes*, May 18, 2023, https:// www.covenanteyes.com/2015/04/10/10-shocking-stats-about-teens-and-pornography/.

Chapter 7—Acceptance: A Home of Grace

1. Christian Smith and Amy Adamczyk, *Handing Down the Faith: How Parents Pass Their Religion on to the Next Generation* (New York: Oxford University Press, 2021), 5 (emphasis added).

Chapter 8—Availability: A Home of Welcome

1. Madeline Levine, *The Price of Privilege* (New York: HarperCollins, 2006), 116.

2. Levine, *The Price of Privilege*, 32

3. Levine, *The Price of Privilege*, 33.

4. Madeline Levine, *Ready or Not: Preparing Our Kids to Thrive in an Uncertain and Rapidly Changing World* (New York: HarperCollins, 2020), 109.

5. Levine, *Ready or Not*, 109.

Chapter 9—Affection: A Home of Warmth

1. Willow Winsham, "Emperor Frankenstein: The Truth Behind Frederick II of Sicily's Sadistic Science Experiments," *History Answers*, August 19, 2017, https://www.historyanswers.co.uk/kings-queens/emperor-frankenstein-the-truth-behind-frederick-ii-of-sicilys-sadistic-science-experiments/

2. Maia Szalavitz, "It's the Orphanages, Stupid!" *Forbes*, April 20, 2010, https://www.forbes.com/2010/04/20/russia-orphanage-adopt-children-opinions-columnists-medialand.html?sh=5d06915621e6.

3. Robert Waldinger and March Schulz, *The Good Life: Lessons from the World's Longest Scientific Study of Happiness* (New York: Simon and Schuster, 2023), 47.

4. Christian Smith and Amy Adamczyk, *Handing Down the Faith: How Parents Pass Their Religion on to the Next Generation* (New York: Oxford University Press, 2021), 2.

5. "Does Your Face Light Up?" *Oprah's Lifeclass*, taped May 26, 2000, https://www.youtube.com/watch?v=9Jw0Fu8nhOc (emphasis added).

Acknowledgments

As I finish this book, I am thankful. The Lord has met me in tender ways along this journey, sustaining me and encouraging me just when I needed it the most. I'm so grateful for his goodness, mercy, and love. He's the reason I have hope.

I'm thankful for encouraging friends who walked alongside me as I wrote. So many friends and family faithfully prayed for this project—thank you especially to my "praying friends" email group. I'm grateful for your encouraging texts, Marco Polos, and Voxer messages. I treasure your friendship and needed every one of your prayers!

I'm also thankful for the wisdom and insight of Sandi Taylor, Mary Kulp, and Winfree Brisley. Thank you for taking the time to read the manuscript and provide helpful feedback. I'm so grateful for each of you and the perspective you offer. I'm also grateful for the support and encouragement of Laura Wifler and Emily Jensen and the entire Risen Motherhood team. Your excitement about this project during our time in Florida spurred me on in my writing.

I'm particularly grateful to Webb and Dowd Simpson for letting me get away to a quiet place and write. I was able to begin this project on one trip and finish the final chapter on another at their lovely home by the lake, with a massive table to be able to spread out all my pages and books. And Dowd, thank you for our walks and being willing to talk with me about all things parenting.

I'm thankful for friends who have given such needed encouragement and advice during this season of writing. Ann Tarwater, thank you and Michael both for your loving support through the years, and especially for the wisdom that began this book. I've prayed "Lord, help me!" multiple times as I've written. Graham and Lisa Cosper, thank you for your faithful friendship. Our getaways to the mountains have refreshed my soul and given me the needed energy and encouragement to write this book. Green house friends—Scott and Karen Friesen, Farr and Kimberly Curlin, Rob and Dottie Bryan—thank you for gifting me with your prayers, your kindness, your encouragement, and your friendships for more than thirty years. Thank you for your excitement and support and prayers for this project from the very beginning.

I have the privilege to work alongside excellent editors, gifted writers, and friends at The Gospel Coalition. These colleagues encourage me as a writer as I read their words and glean from their wisdom. I owe a special thank you to Courtney Doctor and Ann Westrate (as well as their teams) for their faithful prayers for this project. I'm so thankful for your friendship, support, and partnership in ministry.

I am indebted to both Robert Wolgemuth and Austin Wilson for their helpful assistance and advice. They handle all the details of the publishing process so well and give me the freedom to focus on writing. Thank you for all you do.

I've truly enjoyed getting to work with the entire Harvest House team on this project. I'm thankful to Bob Hawkins, Sherrie Slopianka, Audrey Greeson, and Lindsay Lewis for their support, excitement, and encouragement of this book. I'm particularly grateful to Steve Miller and the many hours he spent editing this manuscript as well as offering helpful feedback and advice. His insights and perspective have been such a blessing. Thank you to the entire team for your efforts to get this book into the hands of readers.

My family was incredibly supportive while I was working on this project. My parents, Bob and Anita Bryan, cheer me on in everything I do. I'm so thankful for all the ways they faithfully and lovingly parented me. Thank you for making home such a wonderful place to be—even when I drove the car through the garage door.

My children—Emma, John, and Kate—were ages 22, 19, and 16 as I wrote. I promised not to write too much about them in these pages, but I could write an entire book about how much I admire each one of them. I love having a front-row seat and watching the ways God is working in and through them. They've prayed for me, written loving notes, and cheerfully allowed me to sneak away and spend hours in the office writing. Thank you for giving me the time and encouragement I needed to write this book.

I couldn't do any of the writing I do without the support of my husband, Mike. He prays for me, helps me find time to write, and patiently answers all the theological and biblical questions I regularly send his way. He's my best friend, faithful encourager, and friendly editor—he makes my writing better in every way. He's also been my parenting partner for the past 23 years, and I'm so grateful to be on this journey with him. I couldn't ask for a better dad, and he makes me a better parent. Home is whenever and wherever we're all together.

And to my readers: thank you. So many of you have written me letters of encouragement after reading my other books. Often the notes came to my inbox just when I was feeling discouraged or didn't particularly feel like writing. Thank you for reminding me why I write. As you seek to parent with hope, this is my prayer for you:

> This I call to mind, and therefore I have hope: The steadfast love of the LORD never ceases; his mercies never come to an end; they are new every morning; great is your faithfulness. "The LORD is my portion," says my soul, "therefore I will hope in him" (Lamentations 3:21-24).

Holding on to hope,
Melissa Kruger

A Study Guide That Helps You to Gain More from *Parenting with Hope*

With this study guide companion to *Parenting with Hope*, author and experienced mom of teens Melissa Kruger provides wisdom for navigating the teen years and creating a home environment that encourages teens to grow and mature in their faith—long after they leave.

Using a combination of thought-provoking questions, opportunities for reflection, and practical guidance, Melissa will help you…

- prayerfully study and live out God's Word
- apply scriptural insight as you consider each aspect of your teens' lives: home, church, school, and their social and extracurricular activities
- identify biblical principles and values that will equip and enrich you in your parenting journey

Parenting is not easy, and parenting teenagers comes with a unique set of challenges. This insightful resource will help you think biblically, engage gracefully, and live wisely so that this can be a spiritually formative season of life—for you *and* your teenage children.

To learn more about Harvest House books and
to read sample chapters, visit our website:

www.harvesthousepublishers.com

HARVEST HOUSE PUBLISHERS
EUGENE, OREGON